D1131078

LOTTERIES

LOTTERIES

Alan J. Karcher

Transaction Publishers
New Brunswick (U.S.A.) and London (U.K.)

Library of Congress Catalog Number: 88-37531
ISBN: 0-88738-284-3
Printed in the United States of America

Library of Congress Cataloging-in-Publication Data

Karcher, Alan J.
  Lotteries / Alan J. Karcher.
    p. cm.
  Includes index.
  ISBN 0-88738-284-3
  1. Lotteries—United States.
  2. Advertising—Lotteries—United States. I. Title.
HG6126.K37 1989
336.1'7'0973—dc19   88-37531
                                                        CIP

To my late father, Joseph T. Karcher,
who always thought that writing books was second only to practicing law.
Holding public office was, to him, a distant third.

CONTENTS

Acknowledgments ix

Introduction. 1

PART ONE

1. Past History and Present Comparisons 11
2. Lotteries as a Response to the New Federalism 19
3. The Quick-Fix that Led to Serious Addiction. 27

PART TWO

4. Lotteries as State Tax Policy 37
5. State Lotteries: Grafting Private Enterprise
   onto Government Structures 47
6. Marketing the Lotteries: Present Practices 54
7. Marketing the Lotteries of the Future 64
8. Advertising the Lotteries: Present Practices. 72

PART THREE

9. Tax Reform: Toward a Less Regressive Lottery. 91
10. Budget Process Reform: Pulling in the States' Necks 98
11. Marketing Reform 101
12. Advertising Reform 108

Conclusion 113

Index 117

Acknowledgments

Very special thanks are in order for my friend and former associate, Christopher Guidette. It is both genuine and accurate to say that, without Chris's help, this book would never have been published. He has served tirelessly as both counselor and editor, bringing to the task the same considerable talents he evidenced when he served as Director of Communications for the New Jersey General Assembly during my Speakership. Over the course of those years, Chris and I were in daily contact. In retrospect, I must candidly acknowledge that his advice was always solid, his style sensible, and his judgments mature. So it has been with his advice on this undertaking. I am greatly indebted to Chris for his help, and I particularly appreciate the time he has given in view of the fact that he has moved on from the political scene to an extremely successful career in the private sector. Despite the pressures of that career, he has continued to remain a close friend, counselor, and colleague.

I also wish to thank my wife, Peggy, for her patience, support, and cooperation throughout this endeavor. My daughters, Elizabeth and Ellen, were both working on their Masters degrees during this process, and provided sound advice. Finally, my son, Tim, deserves a special mention for helping me become computer literate.

He was a few paces away from them when suddenly the group broke up and two of the men were in a violent altercation. For a moment they seemed almost on the point of blows.

"Can't you bleeding well listen to what I say? I tell you no number ending in seven ain't won for over fourteen months!"

"Yes it 'as, then!"

"No, it 'as not! Back 'ome I got the 'ole lot of 'em for over two years wrote down on a piece of paper. I takes 'em down reg'lar as the clock. An' I tell you, no number ending in seven—"

"Yes, a seven 'as won! I could pretty near tell you the bleeding number. Four oh seven, it ended in. It were in February—second week in February."

"February your grandmother! I got it all down in black and white. An' I tell you no number—"

They were talking about the Lottery. Winston looked back when he had gone thirty meters. They were still arguing, with vivid, passionate faces. The Lottery, with its weekly pay-out of enormous prizes, was the one public event to which the proles paid serious attention. It was probable that there were some millions of proles for whom the Lottery was the principal if not the only reason for remaining alive. It was their delight, their folly, their anodyne, their intellectual stimulant. Where the Lottery was concerned, even people who could barely read and write seemed capable of intricate calculations and staggering feats of memory. There was a whole tribe of men who made a living simply by selling systems, forecasts, and lucky amulets. Winston had nothing to do with the running of the Lottery, which was managed by the Ministry of Plenty, but he was aware (indeed everyone in the Party was aware) that the prizes were largely imaginary.

—George Orwell, *1984*

Introduction

On November 8, 1988, the voters in Montana, Idaho, Kentucky, and Minnesota approved lotteries for their states, bringing to a total of thirty-three the jurisdictions in the United States that have legalized such operations. If past patterns hold we can predict 1989 sales of lottery tickets to exceed $16 billion, and expect to read, see, and hear $250 million worth of advertising promoting these lotteries. With this amount of money being spent to promote continued and increased wagering on these contests, it is no wonder that we have come to think of lotteries as a widespread, relatively harmless, and perhaps a socially useful form of legalized gambling. This, however, is much too narrow a view.

A lottery is not just another variety of gambling; rather, it is a means of distributing benefits and burdens within a society. The benefits need not be money, nor must the burdens be taxes.

Lotteries have been used as a procedure for allocating a diverse array of benefits, ranging from visas for immigration to the United States right on down to the rights to draft the most talented college basketball players. Recently, when 35,000 people in the eastern United States signed up for the first options to buy 700 moderately priced condominium units, the developer used a lottery system as the fairest method to decide who would get these sought after homes. In California, prospective buyers must take their chances in lottery drawings even when the houses cost half a million dollars. On the other hand, lotteries have been used for distributing burdens such as the obligation for military service, as was the case in the final years of the Vietnam War.

Indeed, lotteries are devices of ancient and honored origin, not for the purpose of gambling money, but for the fair distribution of the good and bad things that must be spread throughout the members of a tribe, clan, state, or nation.

If we want to understand the current lottomania phenomenon, we should first try to understand what lotteries really are all about. Lotteries are a means to an end. In the case of the state-run gambling lotteries the players unquestionably are motivated by the hope that they will get rich quick. But they also view the lottery as an acceptable means to the end that the money wagered collectively by the participants be redistributed in a fair and neutral manner. In other words, the players perceive the lotteries as providing them with a fair chance—a chance that is as fair as the next person's. The states, on the other hand, perceive the end solely to be the raising of revenue, and operate the lotteries

1

with the single motivation of making as much profit as the market will bear. It is these differences in viewpoint and motivation between the states and their citizens that we will focus on to obtain a deeper understanding of the present and future of state-run lotteries.

Nothing in the promotion of lotteries and precious little in the research available to policy makers, who must oversee them, provided any insight into their economic and social consequences. There has been little to guide state officials in guarding against the worst excesses of the state lotteries that, the experience of the past decade begins to suggest, are becoming exploitative of an underclass which participates on a disproportionate level.

Central to this analysis is the examination of lotteries as instruments of state tax policy. As the subject of state tax policy, lotteries are categorized as a "sin tax." Careful examination demonstrates that, if there is any stigma of sin attached to the lotteries, it is presently misplaced. If any stigma is to be placed, it is more appropriate to place it on the states than on the players of the lottery.

Behavioral and ecclesiastical concerns aside, those who aspire to or assume a role in the making of public opinion or public policy must now concern themselves with systems that presently contain greater potential for inflicting social harm than accomplishing social benefits. The lotteries, lacking internal or external oversight, have taken on a life of their own. The revenue generated by the lotteries in this decade has resulted in the states losing perspective on what should legitimately be expected from these games. Worse than lost perspective is the tendency to turn a blind eye toward the real and potential abuses inherent in a system of state-run gambling.

But before we delve deeper into the specific issues involved in the operation of the state-run gambling lotteries, it is useful to examine why lotteries are, in general, widely accepted as the most egalitarian of games.

Philosophers have a name for the issue of "who gets what," and how "give and take" works, or should work, in our society. They call it "distributive justice," and they have been thinking about it for thousands of years. There exists a wide range of options for the distribution of benefits and burdens. Which of those options is fair? Which of those options coincide with our traditional notions of what is just? Is it necessary to use the same system or method for distributing both benefits and burdens, or should we have one method for distributing benefits and an entirely different system for allocating burdens? The use of a lottery is only one option, but it is a popular option for many purposes. Why is this so? The answer may lie in examining some of the other popular options for decision making and seeing how they compare with, yet differ from, the lottery option.

The following is a list of some of the most popular options available to be used in making choices in reference to the distribution of benefits and burdens. Each of these options has enjoyed advocacy by a famous philosopher, who thought that his particular option was the fairest and most just way to allocate both rewards and responsibilities. The list probably could be expanded, but these five appear to be the standard menu. Benefits should be distributed to each, and burdens exacted from each as follows:

1. To each and from each according to his or her merit or virtue.
2. To each and from each according to the contribution he or she makes to the general welfare of the community.
3. To each and from each according to his or her effort.
4. To each and from each according to his or her need.
5. To each and from each an equal share both of the benefits and of the duties of the society.

I referred to this list as a menu because, as a practical matter, our society picks and chooses from this list different options at different times according to the circumstances, and according to our implicit social contracts.

For example, in our society we distribute a whole range of social welfare programs using the "need" option. Public assistance, food stamps, and Medicaid are all programs where we have chosen to use need as the criteria for distribution. On the other hand, free public elementary and secondary education is made available to all, regardless of need. Indeed, all of what we have come to call our fundamental rights (for example, the right to a jury trail, the right to hold property, and the right to freedom of religion) also are distributed pursuant to this "equal share" option.

We use another option, however, when we consider admissions to first-tier universities and medical schools. For these choices we, as a society, have selected to use the "merit" option, reserving coveted spots in these institutions of learning for those who can demonstrate that they are most deserving, based on their previous achievements. The one area of our society where we are most likely to witness a combination of options being exercised simultaneously is in the distribution of wealth. Here we see effort, merit, and service all working together. Of course, there are exceptions to the rule, such as in the case of inheritance, but those members of the society who exert the effort, strive to achieve, and put in the hours are most likely to be rewarded by making the most money. These are, of course, all examples of the distribution of benefits. Let's turn now to examine what options are used in distributing burdens.

Three of the most common burdens are obedience to the general laws, support of the government's operations by taxation, and defense of the country. The first of these obligations, obedience to the law, falls equally upon everyone. The "equality" option is reflected in the maxim that "no one is above the law and no one beneath it." The collection of taxes to support the government's operation reflects the exercise of virtually every option on our list. A per capita, or so-called "head" tax falls equally on all, as do most sales and consumption taxes. On the other hand, tax exemptions are premised on "merit" factors. For example, on the state level, veterans and senior citizens are entitled to certain tax exemptions in recognition of their service to their country. At the core of our systems, both state and federal, is the option to tax in some method that is known as "progressive," which embraces the notion of distributing the burdens in such a manner as to assess obligations according to the individual's ability to pay.

When it comes to military service, however, the "equality" option often goes by the board. Military service in the United States has had a checkered past, with different options being exercised at different times. We have seen voluntary service, universal conscription, "selective service," and, of course, even the lottery option used as methods to distribute the obligations of national defense.

The system used from World War II through the mid-1960s euphemistically was referred to as "selective service," and, indeed, it was selective to say the least. Deferrals and exemptions were granted for young men who were attending college, employed in certain professions (such as teaching and medicine), or married and the father of a child. Every possible loophole in the regulations was used by the creative and the knowledgeable to avoid being drafted for duty in Vietnam. By the mid-1960s combat units were disproportionally composed of the poor, the undereducated, and, of course, minorities. The "selective" option resulted in draft boards selecting out those who were white, educated, and privileged.

Military service based on a lottery system was seen and used as a reasonable and fair alternative to the selective service. The shift to lottery selection was perceived to be much more equitable and won much greater public acceptance. The use of the lottery process halted the accusations of favoritism, primarily because it was seen even as being morally neutral and insulated from all improper influences. In sum, the lottery was viewed as the most egalitarian method for making tough draft decisions.

Aren't these some of the very same reasons that underlie the public's support for state-run gambling lotteries?

Purchase a lottery ticket and you are able to cut yourself free from history, both personal and cosmic. The ticket in your hand gains you entrance into a world that temporarily permits you to forget your heritage, your status, and your educational attainments (or lack thereof). Here wealth doesn't count, nor does occupation, intelligence, connections, merit, or previous service to the welfare of your community. You've entered a realm that is ethically neutral. It makes no difference whether you are noble or ignoble, benevolent or sinister, deserving or undeserving, needy or affluent. You have become absolutely equal to every other participant in the lottery pool—no better and no worse. A lottery ticket is your passport into a world of egalitarian democracy at its most inviting. Hold that ticket in your hand and you are transported to the magic kingdom of fantasy, where that amoral monarch Lady Luck rules. If fate and fortune are with you, that is all that is necessary. In this realm, even the greatest of thinkers, Aristotle, Aquinas, Locke, Kant, and Marx, carry no greater weight nor have any influence greater than the predictions of the writer of the daily horoscope column. But if this is only a fantasy, a dream world, why do millions upon millions of players put up their money day after day?

I suggest that the players keep playing for the very reasons I have just outlined. The players perceive this world of chance and luck as a reasonable, if not sensible, way of redistributing benefits in a manner that is fair and free from the influences that otherwise dominate and control their lives. For the players, this is the option of choice, and that option is exercised every time a lottery ticket is bought. The lottery, on its face, appears to be the quintessential egalitarian institution.

Every time a ticket is bought, the purchaser of that ticket voluntarily steps behind what the contemporary philosopher John Rawls has called "the veil of ignorance." This veil allows those who step behind it to proceed on a level playing field, for the veil blinds the individual to his own talents, merits, efforts, and needs and, more importantly, blinds the player to the talents, merits, efforts, and needs of all others. Life behind this veil is a matter of pure equality. Rawls, in his famous treatise, *A Theory of Justice,* spends a great deal of time and effort speculating on the type of social contract that might be negotiated by those who are behind this veil of ignorance. Perhaps so much speculation was not necessary. The lottery option is demonstrably the choice of millions who choose, daily, to step behind the veil and take their chance on what they believe to be a totally level playing field.

I do not mean to imply that the lottery constitutes some type of Rawlsian paradigm for a system of distributive justice; Rawls's theory is much more complex and sophisticated than that. By the same token, lotteries, particularly in their purest forms, do approach a model system of distributive justice. The purest form of a lottery is one in which each player has an equal chance of winning; that is, no player holds more tickets or chances than any other player, and the entire wagered pool is distributed to the winning players. You are unlikely to observe or participate in such a pure lottery except at a neighbor's house while watching the Super Bowl or the World Series. Ironically, these lotteries, though the fairest, are technically illegal. Certainly, the state-sponsored and -operated lotteries do not (even remotely) resemble pure lottery systems, yet this is not enough of a reason to warrant serious criticism.

In suggesting any criticism of the state-run lottery systems one runs the considerable risk of being considered presumptuous and even patronizing.

After all, the lotteries are voluntary and enjoy wide support among the public. Moreover, this is a free society, and citizens, no matter how poor, should have wide latitude in buying what they choose. This applies most strongly when we are talking about the purchase of a commodity that is not only legal, but actually is sold by the state itself. Paternalism should have no place in a truly free society, and most particularly where a legal, state-authorized commodity is involved.

If criticisms are to be leveled they had best be strong and even more strongly justified. Bearing this in mind, I will try to set forth exactly what is wrong with our present state-run lottery systems, and to suggest what should be done to cure the existing problems. To make it absolutely clear from the beginning, the targets of my criticism are not the players. If anything, they are often victims of a system that has been twisted and distorted by the very governments that are supposed to be protecting them from victimization.

My first criticism centers on the disparity of perception between players and state. Players view lotteries as having as their purpose, or end, the fair and equitable redistribution of money. The state views lotteries as a method of raising money without having to acknowledge or defend the level of the actual tax. This disparity of perception as to the purpose of the lotteries is not the problem. The problem arises out of the fact that people support lotteries as a fair, attractive, and egalitarian form of risk-taking. To have this "fair game" made legally available the people must deal with a state monopoly that exacts an aggregate tax of 50 percent—the highest tax levied on anything anywhere in the United States. The states then attempt to justify this high tax by labeling it a "sin tax."

If the disparity of perception as to the ends of the lottery leads to a regressive, and what some would call an obnoxious, level of taxation, the disparity between the way the players view the process and the way the state treats the process of the lottery procedure leads to a situation that verges on the outrageous. While the players (the high odds notwithstanding) do not merely accept, but welcome, the opportunity to place themselves on the level playing field behind the veil of ignorance, the state remains conspicuously outside the veil.

The state, far from seeking blind participation on a level playing field, instead attempts to know everything it can about the players. The state routinely studies the age, sex, race, educational levels, buying habits, residences, and income levels of not only existing players, but of all the potential players as well. The state does this so that it can utilize this information to create advertising campaigns, place ticket outlets, and manipulate the entire promotional operation of its enterprise so as to squeeze more and more dollars out of the players, present and future.

In summary, we find a gaping chasm between the state and its citizens. The players see the lottery as a means, characterized by its neutrality and freedom from historical and cultural differences, to obtain a fair chance to see money redistributed, hopefully to themselves. But, if the money does not come to them, at least they know that they had a fair chance, and that the money wagered was redistributed in a just and even-handed manner. In essence, the players see the lottery as an egalitarian institution, and also as a system insulated from improper influences. The state, on the other hand, views the lottery merely as a means of utilizing sophisticated marketing techniques to manipulate and encourage ever-increasing participation in a system whose end is to raise as much revenue as possible.

The end result is a system that, as tax policy, is regressive and rapacious, that uses promotions that target the poor, and that markets tickets in a manner that is often abusive and exploitative. These, indeed, are the three "sins" of the states: avarice, conscious oppression of the poor, and hypocrisy.

These are strong charges, but I am prepared to defend them in clear terms that will demonstrate the need for changes in the way the states currently are operating their lotteries.

Part One of this work examines the histories, both ancient and modern, of lotteries. This work also examines how our lotteries compare to traditional lotteries and how these games are conducted in other parts of the world. We will then take a look at how Reaganomics and its "fend-for-yourself federalism" has given the states impetus to rely increasingly on lotteries as fundraising mechanisms. Finally, we assess the present lottery revenues to the various states to determine how large a role they play in their respective budget pictures.

In Part Two, we examine the marketing of lotteries in various states. A great deal of attention is devoted to how and where the states decide to locate ticket outlets. We look at the way state lottery agencies view their role. Is their job to regulate, or to sell tickets? Finally, in Part Two, we look at the important question of who is responsible for the advertising and marketing plans, and how the decision is made as to whether or not a given approach is in good taste and not exploitative. Is the message measured by its objectivity and fairness, or solely by its likelihood to generate more sales?

Part Three focuses on some suggested changes in the way the states are presently doing business, and includes recommended reforms. These recommendations are an attempt to balance the reality of the continuing existence of the lottery in over half the states and its probable expansion into others, with the goal of having the operations run in a manner that adequately mirrors our inherent values of fair play.

PART I

1

Past History and Present Comparisons

Lotteries and the function of chance have long held a special fascination for authors of both fiction and nonfiction. Western literature is filled with references to lotteries. From sacred scripture to the modern American novelist, John Updike, references to lotteries and the way they can transform the lives of winners abound.

American writers recount how Thomas Jefferson fell under the lottery spell when, in an uncharacteristic flip-flop, he changed his mind about supporting one. Jefferson, who originally expressed strong reservations about the moral rectitude of raising money from gambling, later became a convert to the value of lotteries as the growing country's economic necessities softened his resistance.

In a report for the fiscal year of 1982–1983, issued by the Commonwealth of Pennsylvania, can be found a full page devoted to "Lotteries: Past and Present," which not only advised the reader of the biblical citations, but went into detail about lotteries as sales-promotions devices in sixteenth century Italy, and concluded with the tidbit that the Republican Party platform of 1957 called for a national lottery. One of its most remarkable disclosures is that the Chase National Bank of New York was originally capitalized by means of a lottery.

The Report of the New Jersey State Lottery Planning Commission, published in 1970, invoked the Bible and ancient Rome, and revealed that lotteries were conducted as entertainment at Roman banquets. Here also can be found an account of the demise of the infamous Louisiana State Lottery in the latter part of the nineteenth century.

While rich in color, the majority of this predictable and extensive historical material is always unsatisfactory. No conclusion is ever reached other than to indicate that lotteries have precedents in history. All of the information is, for the most part, irrelevant, because it is never pulled together to support a meaningful statement about why lotteries enjoy widespread patronage; or why they have been, and are presently, viewed as fair methods of leveling an uneven

11

world. Perhaps all of the authors who provide a selective litany of the precedents believe that the information is, in itself, sufficient, and that the inductive processes of the readers will inexorably lead to some personal conclusion.

The Bible dignifies, the ancient Romans justify, and the American tradition legitimizes the lotteries without ever comparing those lotteries with the present-day state-run games of chance.

This is not to say that history is merely interesting but not inevitably instructive. History, when assembled into rational argument, can both teach and persuade. Mere recitation of precedent does neither. Something new is needed in the literature of lotteries. An analysis of the historical data in terms of what it says about human nature, and about lotteries on the rational, ethical, and even biological levels, would be useful. What is needed is a science of lotteries, at least within the context of Jules Henri Poincaré's famous admonition that "science is built up with facts, as a house is built up with stones. But a collection of facts is no more a science than a heap of stones is a house." To date, all of the voluminous data on lotteries has remained as a heap of stones.

A review of the history suggests lotteries are not the product of avarice, but of man's innate desire to absolve himself of moral responsibility. At their core, lotteries are an egalitarian and rational way to free decision-making from improper influences. They are, moreover, an ethical means of allowing divine intervention to manifest itself without obligating the victor, or stigmatizing the loser. Finally, when viewed in the context of Darwin's theory of natural selection, they are the unspoken but controlling principle of existence itself.

Let us look at each of the major historical traditions of the lottery separately, starting with an examination of the way lotteries were used to insulate political decisions from improper influences. We then move to consideration of the ethical implications of choice by lottery. Finally, we look at how deeply ingrained in us is our positive response to lottery methodology.

George Luis Borges's short story, "The Lottery in Babylon," first appeared in an American edition in 1964. The story involves a mythical state in which all decisions, on every level, are made by the use of a lottery. A citizen in Borges's kingdom can find himself impoverished and imprisoned one day, only to be elevated to the status of wealthy ruler on the next day. Everything, including life and death, is the proper subject matter of the luck of the draw. The realm described by this Nobel laureate isn't that far-fetched. There is evidence that some leadership positions, particularly in aristocracies, were selected by lot. For example, this was the manner by which public offices rotated in Athens in the age of Pericles. In fact, the system was not only interesting in its operation, but equally fascinating in its conception. The Periclean arrangement could best be described as "king for a day." This process offered each and every citizen the same equal and random opportunity to preside over the Council, or lower house of the legislature, for a day at a time. The selection was by lot, and the aim of the process was to eliminate corruption. Even the temptation of bribery was removed by waiting until the very last moment to determine which committee of the Council, and, specifically, which member of that committee, would preside for the day. The presiding officer had very broad powers, but they lasted only for that day. Since the members of the Council initially were chosen by lot, and an additional lottery was used to refine down to the daily leader, it clearly was possible for any citizen to become the "first citizen" of the city, at least for a brief period.

The concept of trial by jury goes back to the first great lawgiver in western civilization. Solon, a man whose very name has become a synonym for lawmaker, instituted a number of reforms in Athens in 594 B.C. Perhaps the most famous of those reforms was the creation of the jury system that provided for the "admission of the lowest class of the citizens to full parity with the highest classes in being eligible for selection to the 'heliaea'." This body was, in fact, a "pool" of six thousand potential jurors that, in turn, were summoned forth by lot to sit and decide on all cases except those involving capital crimes; that is, murder and treason. Juries today are selected in much the same way. All registered voters or/and licensed drivers who are citizens are eligible for service as jurors. The initial summoning to the court is by a lottery system, and then actual seating on a particular jury is again a matter of each individual being chosen by lot. The highest placed, richest, and most powerful are subject to being called to duty as are the most humble.

What this demonstrates is that lotteries were widely and happily accepted by the Greeks as a way of insuring that no one could possibly abuse their political or financial influence. However, it was really more complex than just insulating the system from corrupting pressures; this was a system that allowed equals to distribute both obligations and benefits in a manner that was neutral in all respects. The king for the day as well as the chosen juror brought to his duties no obligations of friendship or favor. He was there because of the luck of the draw. By the same token, the person passed over carried no shame. It was not that he was unworthy or disliked, or even distrusted or unsuited, merely unlucky. We see this very same attitude today in the distribution of certain other obligations besides jury duty. The military draft is just one other example. Even the allocation of medical services have been the subject matter of choice by lottery. As recently as 1987, lotteries were under active and serious consideration as a suitable manner by which to determine who would receive critical organ transplants. Who shall live and who shall die is as grave a matter of human decision as there is. But the logic of choice by lottery was very compelling, and the lottery was seriously advanced as a fair way of making that decision. The person denied the life-sustaining transplant dies not because he is unworthy. It is not a question of being undeserving or meritless, just a question of luck. On the other side of the equation is the survivor who attains that enviable status, not as the result of influence or power, but simply as a matter of good fortune. The survivor didn't cheat anyone and need not live out the balance of his extended life beholden to anyone or with feelings of guilt toward anyone. On the level playing field of choice by lottery, they just happened to win.

Just as our modern society looks to the ancient world of Athens for our intellectual and rational traditions, its ethical traditions are rooted in the Judaic–Christian teachings. In both the Old and New Testaments we find strong endorsements of choice by lot.

Many will recall that there were twelve original apostles, and that when Judas hung himself the group was left one man short. Two names were put forward, and after much prayer lots were drawn, and Matthias was chosen. The full text reads as follows, "And they put forward two: Joseph, called Barsabbas, who was surnamed Justus, and Matthias. And they prayed and said, 'Thou, Lord, who knowest the hearts of all, show which of these two Thou hast chosen to take the place in this ministry and apostleship from which Judas fell away to go to his own place.' And they drew lots between them, and the lot fell upon Matthias; and he was numbered with the eleven apostles."

Of course, what is illustrated here is the reliance that those of faith have in a lottery as a means of Divine Providence exercising a choice in human affairs. It must be noted that the Bible is silent as to which of the two candidates had worked the hardest or was most devoted. Nor does it speak to their training, their aptitude, or years of service. To the nonbelieving, the choice of Matthias is a matter of pure luck of the draw; but to the vast majority of the faithful, this report gave credence over the last two millennia that the Lord, "who knowest the hearts of all," would use this system to make His decisions as to who should prosper and who should fail. Here the lottery operates in a manner that is neutral in value. No aspersion is cast on the loser; he need not slink off with his head down, having been judged to be unworthy. Nor could Matthias claim exceptional virtue or have any reason to be proud. He won as a result of the Lord's will, and not for any other reason. The mystical ways of heaven result in peaceful resolution of potential conflict on earth.

Two important points are therefore established by this biblical text:

(1) The historical acceptance of selection by lottery, as a value-neutral method of distributing or allocating benefits and burdens; and
(2) That the lottery as a morally correct method of distribution and allocation of benefits and burdens was divinely sanctioned.

There are a total of twenty-one references to the choice by lot within the Bible. Of these, eighteen are contained in the Old Testament, and none are more profound than the following lines from Proverbs 16:33, "The lots may be cast into the lap, but the issue depends wholly on the LORD." What exactly does this mean? On one level it is rather straightforward, and refers to the same attitude that was reflected in the last citation concerning the selection of Matthais. The choice by lot is controlled by Divine Providence not by any of the normal factors and influences, proper or improper, that we must all normally contend with. What could be more fair? What could be more morally comfortable? But on another level a deeper message may be read into this translation. A message is here that strikes something in the collective unconscious, something that is archetypal and speaks literally and figuratively at the genetic level. Isn't this proverb actually a metaphor for reproduction? (The Hebraic dictionary indicates that the word translated as "lap" can as easily be translated as pocket or womb.) And isn't the act of reproduction the greatest lottery that ever existed, and likely to keep that status?

The male genes are as lots being cast into the lap-womb of the female, where there are virtually billions of potential recombinations possible. Chance recombinant DNA is the ultimate gamble and what the human race is today is the ultimate payoff of the gambles that thousands of generations have been taking as to the issue of this casting of lots into laps.

What does this add to the history of lotteries? It says something about the appreciation and acceptance of the function of chance that is pervasive in our culture. We all understand, deep down, at the most basic level of our existence, that we ourselves are the products of chance, and that we differ from our parents, from our siblings, and from everyone else in a fashion that has occurred as the result of this universal and historical genetic lottery. The very fact that we exist as a species separate and apart from others is a factor of evolutionary contingency. Indeed, since life itself appeared on this planet hundreds of millions of years ago there has been a continuing lottery of genetic material going on, with only God having any knowledge or control over the "issue."

The history of lotteries, therefore, teaches us that this system of decision-making is not merely time honored, it is literally in our very bones. What other system of choice can make even the remotest claim to enjoying such a solid foundation? The acceptance of this methodology for resolving questions of distributing benefits or allocating risks and burdens has the legal, political, and rational precedent of ancient Greece's governmental theory. Lotteries clearly also have enjoyed the ethical and religious approval that can only be given by the Bible with its assurances that this is a manner in which God works His will here on earth. Finally, on top of this already prestigious pedigree, lotteries have the biological parallel; indeed, it is more than just an analog, it is life itself that we recognize as the greatest of all lotteries. Can there be any doubt as to why lotteries are readily accepted, and, in fact, welcomed?

Obviously, the history of lotteries may be viewed in a much more significant way than as a mere recitation of dates, places, and events. The common threads of the long precedents are not that they dignify or legitimize this manner of decision-making, but that they tell us something about ourselves. We are the only species that is both reflective and judgmental. We seek methods of conflict resolution that are rational in their exclusion of improper influences and ethical in their neutrality. We choose to make decisions by lot because that method absolves the individuals from personal responsibility, either for victory or defeat. Ultimately, we understand that our very lives are the products of chance. We did not need education, wealth, influence, merit, or effort. Our existence was solely the result of luck of the draw.

Lotteries are an extremely fair means of decision-making in certain situations. If a level playing field is the objective, if moral neutrality is desired, if a method of resolving conflict without stigmatizing the loser or lauding the winner is the objective, then lotteries are an excellent means of selection.

The state lotteries in operation today are a far cry from what we have just reviewed. The print media for state lotteries are usually dominated by a huge and ubiquitous dollar sign. Television commercials for these state lotteries depict such themes as a woman sticking her tongue out at her employer after announcing news of her lottery win. Radio jingles encourage buying tickets on the inducement that "fairy tales can come true."

Visit the most distressed area of your state's poorest city and you will quickly witness what the lotteries in America have become. Look into the faces of those who line up at the terminals to buy tickets, counting the change in their pockets as the devout count the beads on a rosary. The tickets that they buy tax their dreams and their hopes. If this is really entertainment, why does no one seem amused? If this is recreation, then why is the mood so sullen and abject? Haven't we lost something important in our over-commercialization of the lotteries?

Where have we gone wrong? As with many other institutions, the lottery is a device that is easily subject to abuse. In fact, at the heart of the indictment of the present gambling lotteries must be the charge that the states have used the positive attitudes that people hold toward this form of decision-making, and channeled it into ways to feed the state's growing avarice. The attractiveness of the lotteries' superficial fairness to the individual risk-taker becomes more and more distorted as the process expands and is magnified. And, of course, the pervasive element perverting the process is the profit factor, a factor grown so large that it has addicted the sponsors of the lotteries and blinded them to the problems that must inexorably arise when democratic institutions lose perspective on their role and on their responsibility to their citizens.

The perversion of lotteries by the profit factor is not a universal affliction, it is a malady that appears to be somewhat unique to North American lotteries.

The urge to take chances, and the willingness to risk a little money on the luck of the draw, is, indeed, a trait of human nature pursued worldwide. Lotteries are the peoples' games of choice, whether it be gambling habits in western nations or in Soviet-bloc countries that we are observing.

Lotteries are operated in a hundred nations and on every continent, with the exception of Antarctica. The People's Republic of China launched its lottery in the summer of 1987, with sales reported as being brisk in the ten regions that were used as test markets. The game had been banned since 1949, when it was declared by chairman Mao Zedong to be decadently capitalistic.

The story of the lottery as it is played in other nations is as varied and fascinating as the history of the game itself. But the purpose of this discussion is to focus on how an institution that has been viewed as a game throughout history and is treated as a game everywhere else has been abused on our continent and turned into a strictly business venture by the states.

The common denominators missing from our state-operated lotteries, but generally associated with both the tradition and the current standards of the games throughout the balance of the world, are:

1. Lotteries are viewed as games first and foremost, with revenue-raising seen as nice, but strictly secondary.
2. Lotteries are viewed as a way of creating jobs with little, if any, interest in automating the systems in a way that would eliminate employment.
3. Lotteries are often connected with sporting events or a series of athletic contests.
4. Lotteries are often scheduled to coincide with special festivals or holidays.
5. Lotteries are designed and structured to pay out many small prizes, with large jackpots an occasional rarity. In fact, in communist countries the largest prizes are measured in mere thousands of dollars, not enough to allow even the largest prize winner to lose his socialist perspective.
6. Lotteries advertise in a way which complements the work ethic rather than denigrates the value of labor. A winner is portrayed as being able to take an extra vacation or buy a new car, not thumb his nose at the boss.
7. Lotteries are for the most part enterprises operated independent of the government, but licensed, regulated, and overseen by the government. Indeed, with the rare exception, totally state-run operations are confined to the United States and communist countries.
8. Lotteries are basically social in nature, as opposed to economic. Moreover, gambling is seen as natural, not as a "sin" to which a high penalty, in the form of a high tax, must be attached. Once again, the bias toward viewing lottery gaming as tolerated, but highly taxed, sin seems to be unique to the United States and the communist countries.

18   Lotteries

Ultimately, the majority of recommendations contained in the final chapters of this book will concentrate on how to get our state-run lotteries back into the mainstream of history and tradition.

2

Lotteries as a Response to the New Federalism

While 1987 tax collections rose in the majority of states, tax revenues actually dropped in seven states, and were relatively stagnant in others. The nationwide average increase was 8.3 percent, which was well above the rate of general inflation. The average increase occurred despite sizable declines in some states which pulled down the average, and one very large state, Texas, having a gain of less than 1 percent.

The seven states which experienced a revenue decline were Alaska, Wyoming, Oklahoma, North Dakota, Louisiana, Montana, and West Virginia. Alaska's revenues dropped 43.2 percent, and Wyoming's fell 20.6 percent. What two things do these seven states and the revenue-stagnant state of Texas all have in common? Oil and gas dependency and long-standing traditions of resistance to state-run lotteries are the common denominators. Of these eight states only West Virginia and Montana presently have a lottery, and they are among the most recent to adopt state systems. In each of the remaining states on the list the adoption of lottery legislation is being debated hotly and advanced by ardent advocates, who argue that the adoption of a state lottery will, at least, help close their existing budget gaps. The second attempt in recent years to pass a lottery referendum in North Dakota was rejected by the voters on June 14, 1988. Despite the fact that the margin of defeat was even greater this time, proponents for a lottery were busy the very next day picking up the pieces and marshaling their resources for a third effort to get the state to adopt a lottery. It should be mentioned that North Dakota's governor vigorously opposed the proposition, citing the fact that lotteries victimize the poor.

If any of the other states from this list act to implement a lottery during the present legislative session, they will not be unique in the motivation that brought them to take action in this regard. The chill sting of penury has been the catalyst for the decisions in most of the other states as well. In this chapter we review the dynamics that lead states to make the choice to have a state-run lottery.

The economic imperatives which lead to the initiation of a lottery are only part of the story. Many lottery operations were already in place when the Reagan revolution began. But now all the systems, young or mature, can be said to have flourished as a response to the "fend-for-yourself federalism" of the 1980s.

Taken as a whole, the evidence that emerges is rather compelling proof that a direct cause-and-effect relationship can be established between the policies of Reaganomics and the intensiveness of lottery activity. This is not to say that the lottery was a panacea. Every state has been forced to increase one or more taxes; for many states, lotteries were the easiest revenue-raiser to put in place, with political risks minimized.

In fact, an analysis of all fifty states shows that 300 separate tax increases were enacted in the period between 1981 and 1988. These were offset by very few decreases. Moreover, these increases at the state level do not include local and county increases. Many states, faced with a cutback in federal aid, responded either by inaugurating a state lottery, or by rapidly expanding the promotion of the lottery if one was already in place. The expanded promotion of existing lotteries could easily be seen in such things as increased advertising, additional terminal installations, and, above all else, offering new and different games to the betting public. Lotteries and lottomania have been the states' most regressive response to Reaganomics.

Even today, as states such as Texas and Alaska debate the wisdom of adopting a lottery in their jurisdiction, we are seeing the consequences of the federal policies that bear the indelible mark of the Reagan Administration. Whereas the direct cutbacks in federal aid were felt most immediately in the Northeastern industrialized states such as New York and Massachusetts, it is now states such as Texas and Louisiana which are suffering the consequences of the deregulation of gas and oil, coupled with an international policy that protects shipping in the Persian Gulf, thereby subsidizing the price of foreign oil.

Ronald Reagan took the oath of office as president of the United States in January 1981. The gross sales figures for all lotteries then in existence for their fiscal years ending on June 30, 1980, were $2.4 billion. The figure for gross sales for the fiscal year ending June 30, 1988, will be close to $15 billion. In 1980, there were fourteen states operating lotteries. The 650 percent increase in gross sales in the short course of eight years has, in part, been made possible by the incredible number of additional states that have opted to operate lotteries of their own. That, of course, is a major part of the story, but there is another element to the equation that must be looked at carefully. The last budget submitted by President Carter to Congress provided that 14 percent of every dollar collected at the federal level be returned to the states and/or counties and towns in the form of federal aid. The amount of aid contained in the budget sent to Congress by President Reagan in 1988 was only a little over 9.5 percent of the total budget, $14 billion less than the amount of federal aid appropriated in 1981 in constant dollars. Had federal allocations for state and local aid remained at a steady 14 percent over the course of the Reagan Administration, the dollars flowing back to the states, counties, and municipalities would have been $153 billion. The Reagan revolutionaries have earmarked only $119 billion in the 1988 federal budget for distribution as state and local aid. While the defense component of the budget was growing by 45 percent in the period of 1981-1988, and net interest costs on the national debt were exploding past all other expenses, growing at the rate of 72 percent over the same period, state and local aid fell by 13 percent as reflected in constant dollars. The pressure on state officials represented by these numbers was enormous.

Moreover, the pressure on state budgets caused by the drastic cutbacks in federal aid was compounded by relentless increases in the demand for service levels that were not merely stable, but mounting annually.

State officials seemed to be intrigued with the prospect of being able to raise revenues without offending the sensibilities of an electorate that had become advocates of the tax-cutting hysteria then rampant in many quarters. The Reagan era will have witnessed the more than doubling of the number of jurisdictions playing the lottery. It is not just coincidence that as federal aid decreased, lottery activity increased.

For those states that had already played their lottery card, it was necessary to boost their revenue stream as much as possible. This was accomplished both by the introduction of new games and by substantial increases in expenditures earmarked for advertising and promotion.

The genesis of the lottery in every state is unique, but in many states that adopted lotteries before the advent of the new federalism certain characteristics could be identified. For example, a number of the pre-Reagan-era lottery states are noted for their resistance to the imposition of a state income tax. New Hampshire, which was the first state to introduce the lottery in 1964, and Connecticut, which was the fourth state to adopt a lottery in 1972, have yet to adopt an income tax. Other early lottery states adopted this game as a means of raising revenues before adopting income taxes. The lottery was considered an attempt to stave off the need for a more progressive or broader-based tax.

In New Jersey, the existence of the lottery was actually an obstacle to the adoption of an income tax, as opponents of that tax persisted in their claims that the lottery hadn't yet reached its full potential, and that when it did, there would be no need for an income tax.

The decline of aging industries in New York, Massachusetts, Ohio, and Illinois caused severe economic conditions in these states during the 1970s, and revenue officials were anxious for anything that remotely resembled a viable source of needed funds. Ironically, the economies of these states are on the upswing while many of the wealthiest states of the 1970s, such as Texas and Louisiana, are now on the top of the lists of distressed areas.

Whatever the relative positions of the states in the last decade or in the present, another problem looms for even those states that chose to rely on progressive and supposedly elastic income taxes. Toward the end of 1986, an apparently sophisticated public moved quickly to take advantage of the more favorable capital-gains tax that would no longer be available after January 1987. As a result, many states experienced a sizable jump in their income-tax receipts on returns filed in 1987. The figures for 1988 remain problematic, but all fiscal analysts predict that the new tax code, coupled with the effects of the market crash of October 1987, will result in income tax shortfalls for the states' revenue pictures in 1989.

The present circumstances lend support to predictions that every state will have its own lottery by the year 1995. Certainly, the pressures are there; however, what is of most concern to us at the moment is not speculation about what the future may hold, but rather an in-depth analysis of the impact of fend-for-yourself federalism on lottery activity, both in those states that made the choice in the 1980s and those that already had a lottery in place when the impact of Reaganomics hit.

Two of the largest states without lotteries as of January 1981 were California and Florida. Both were positioned to withstand extraordinary pressures, having stronger-than-average growth rates, diverse economies, no heavy reliance on declining manufacturing bases that were approaching obsolescence, and dependable incomes from oil and gas extraction taxes. Notwithstanding the inherent strengths of their economies and depths of their respective tax bases, both states rapidly felt the impact of the new federal policies. Just as quickly, the voices of those who considered the lottery to be the simplest answer rose in a chorus, advocating immediate adoption of state-operated games.

The governor of California resisted the lottery fever to no avail. The voters of that state knew what they wanted, and after their endorsement of the initiative the governor was actually sued by one group who claimed that he was dragging his feet in putting the lottery into operation.

In Florida, the picture was somewhat different. Historically a low-service state, for decades Florida had attracted retirees with promises of low taxes, no inheritance tax, and no income tax. A public school system that was notoriously inadequate and an infrastructure that was always far behind expectations did not seem to bother anybody, until suddenly everyone woke up at the same time to recognize that the situation had become intolerable and that, if nothing else, the long-deferred maintenance of the infrastructure had to be addressed or bridges might collapse, water faucets go dry, and sewerage run higher than a hurricane tide. An income tax was anathema, and Florida has opted for a lottery as a part of an overall strategy of staving off the need for a progressive, broad-based tax.

These are just two examples of what happened in states feeling the first effects of the federal cutbacks. Over the course of the last seven years every state has suffered from federal cutbacks. Some have adjusted better than others, but the impact has been dramatic. As the effects were felt, each state was forced to weigh its options. The lottery option was only one such option, but for sixteen states it has become an option that has been exercised.

Those in the business of supplying material and equipment to the states for the operation of lotteries were particularly active in encouraging states to exercise the lottery option. For instance, Scientific Games, Inc., a subsidiary of Bally Manufacturing, as part of their efforts to promote the lottery in the nonplaying states, prepared graphic evidence of what states could expect from a lottery. Let's focus on a chart Scientific Games prepared in 1984, at the height of the cutback crisis. The chart, which appeared as a full-page ad in various magazines distributed to state officials, had the headline, IS YOUR STATE LOSING ITS SHARE OF $3,200,000,000? It placed beneath this headline a map of the fifty states showing what each of the states that had not yet adopted a lottery might expect by way of revenue if it implemented a lottery. Underneath the map the text read,

A well-run state-controlled and state-operated Lottery can generate significant new voluntary revenues to meet the revenue needs of state governments. In 1983, the 18 established lotteries (including the District of Columbia) generated over $6,000,000,000 in gross revenues ($62.63 per capita) and approximately $2,400,000,000 in net revenues for their 95,800,000 citizens. Similar performance by the 33 non-lottery states would generate approximately $8,092,000,000 in annual gross revenues and $3,237,000,000 in annual net revenues (40%). The annual net revenues for each of the 33 non-lottery states is shown above in millions of dollars.

Sure enough, numbers appeared inside the states on the map, such as $593 in California, $66 in Oregon, $244 in Florida, and $123 in Missouri. The text continues with this invitation, "Scientific Games will be pleased to provide state officials with detailed information, revenue projections, expert testimony, and model legislative bills for state operated lotteries...Contact Robert L. Mote, General Counsel."

Apparently, if one contacted Mr. Mote, he would give the same answers that he prepared for an article published in May 1984. In fact, the article was entitled "Questions and answers about a state lottery." One of the questions Mr. Mote had posed to himself was, "Is a state-run lottery the answer to the economic problems currently facing my state?" The answer to this question was as follows: "That depends on the severity of the problem. Certainly a state-run lottery is not the answer to all of the financial ills that any state may face at any time. At the same time, in many states the lottery has stabilized state taxes. [Examples are then given.] All of this revenue is raised voluntarily. Needless to say, there are people who oppose lotteries or gambling in any form —these people are free not to buy tickets."

It is best left to a class in communications to dissect this question and answer in its entirety, but it should be pointed out that at the time it was published the problem of revenue shortfalls was assumed. Only the degree of "severity" was relative. This was not really a skillful manipulation of the language so much as it was an accurate statement of the conditions extant in state treasuries in May 1984.

The ads, in combination with the economic pressures, were persuasive. The complexion of the map in the ads in 1988 has changed, with 30 states now indicated as lottery playing and only 20 showing as holdouts.

The economic storm warnings had, in fact, gone up much earlier than when this article appeared in 1984. As the Reagan administration was getting underway in January 1981, the signals were already so clear that in that month *Public Gaming* magazine ran a story entitled "The Economic Potential of State Lotteries." The story gave an opening assessment of the present mood in Washington as follows: "The signal has already come from Washington that there will be a dramatic shift away from the unabated growth in federal spending and taxation. Yet in terms of individual states' finances, in many instances, current economic conditions and federal cut backs have raised havoc with most states' attempts at balancing their budgets." The lottery is suggested as the potential solution for the governors described by the article as "anxiously seeking new revenues."

To some extent, the lottery was in the right place at the right time. Indeed, while not as many states opted for immediate adoption as was predicted by the article (sixteen), the number grew steadily year by year. By 1988, the projected number had become a reality, but the number of dollars collected grew in the early years of the 1980s much more dramatically than did the number of states with legalized state-operated games.

Between 1981 and 1983 only three jurisdictions adopted lotteries, yet gross revenues nationwide doubled. The three additional jurisdictions implementing lottery operations in this two-year time period were the District of Columbia, Colorado, and Washington. The addition of these three, relatively small jurisdictions certainly could not account solely for the huge increase in gross sales. To give an adequate account of this amazing phenomenon, we must find some factor other than the fact that lotteries were now lawful in 18, and opposed to 15, jurisdictions. It is important to point out that while the lottery states were a minority at the time when compared to the nonlottery states, they still represented nearly half the population of the country, and they were as hard pressed as their sister jurisdictions for more revenue. The only difference was that they already had lotteries in place. The answer to why gross receipts jumped so dramatically in these first two years of the new federalism lies in how the states already playing the game responded to the challenge to increase the profits from their existing operations. The answer can be given in one word: LOTTO.

Lotto was a game long known to Europeans and South Americans but only introduced to American lottery players in 1978, when it first appeared in New York. This variation of the game involves the player picking six numbers out of a range of 40 or more numbers. The odds on picking 6 out of 52 numbers (the most common and popular variant of the game) are approximately one in 14 million, and the chances of being struck by lightning are seven times better. The odds notwithstanding, the game, after appropriate publicity, became extremely popular. New Jersey followed New York's lead and instituted the lotto game in 1980, with the other states finally catching up in the 1981–1983 period. Pennsylvania's experience illustrates the meteoric rise in lotto sales. In the first year of lotto availability, fiscal year 1982, lotto sales in Pennsylvania were a little over $12 million. Sales for fiscal year 1983 increased by 1500 percent, to over $185 million. These figures are not unusual. In fact, the story was much the same in every state that made the new game available. Between 1981 and 1982 the lotto provided in a large measure for the over-70-percent increase in gross sales in New York and Ohio and over 50 percent in Illinois. Increases in the range of 25 percent occurred in New Jersey and Massachusetts in the same period. The increases between 1982 and 1983 were equal to or greater than the initial burst of growth.

By the close of business, for the fiscal year 1985, lotto sales had eclipsed sales of the daily three-digit games. The growth in the period of 1983–1985 continued to surge. From gross sales of $689 million reported at the close of 1983, lotto sales surged nationwide to $3.6 billion at the end of fiscal year 1985. This was a quarter of a billion dollars more than revenue realized by all three-digit games produced, despite the fact that in 1983 those daily number games had an existing sizable sales base of almost $3 billion.

Another important trend is identifiable in states that had lotteries prior to the impact of the New Federalism. These states discovered the power of television. Not only was more money allocated for advertising in general as the new lotto game increasingly was seen as the salvation of the lotteries, but television became the dominant medium for promoting the game. In chapter 8 we take a closer look at the major advertising policies that are presently used.

A third dimension of the lotto growth was the exponential growth of outlet terminals both in the mature and in young lottery states. New Jersey had fewer than 2,000 "on-line terminals" in 1980, but by 1987 that number had more than doubled to 4,200. Illinois, which had only 1,000 "on-line terminals" in 1982, put 3600 into operation by 1987, and Washington, which opened its operation in 1984 with 550 terminals, had increased that number to over 1,000 by the beginning of 1988. In chapter 6 we focus intensely on the marketing practices of the lottery operations, and in chapter 7 we look at future marketing possibilities.

The Reagan years have been characterized by painful cutbacks in state and local aid. What we have seen in partial response to those federal policies has been more states playing lotteries, more games, more terminals, more advertising, more reliance on a speculative source of revenue, and more distortion of the lottery tradition.

In the next chapter, we turn our attention to just how large and profitable lotteries have become, and just how reliant states have become on this source of revenue. We also take a look at what some have been saying about the reliability of future growth projections for the lotteries.

3

The Quick-Fix that Led to Serious Addiction

In 1964, New Hampshire started its sweepstakes. New York and New Jersey followed suit, adopting lotteries by 1970. During the following decade other states, primarily in the New England and Mid-Atlantic region, jumped on the lottery bandwagon. The last eight years have witnessed a major expansion of activity with sixteen additional states opting for lotteries, and every state adopting "on-line terminals" to provide more exotic games such as lotto. Three reasons explain this intensification of lottery activity:

1. New revenue needs. Faced with federal cutbacks and escalating expenditures, state after state opted for the lottery's enticing prospect of "painless revenue" raising.
2. Ronald Reagan's rhetoric. The president's advocacy of tax cuts at every level made it increasingly difficult for state lawmakers to discuss more progressive alternatives. The lottery option became, for many elected state officials, not only the first choice, but the only viable and politically realistic alternative. This is not to say that the states were not forced to make tough decisions; they were, and they responded by adopting a wide array of taxes. Some 300 new taxes were adopted or increased in all of the states combined. It is not unreasonable to conclude, however, that many of these tax hikes were lower than they might have been in the absence of the lottery alternative.
3. Unexpected results. The lotto game, which was being played in all the lottery states by 1983, proved to be an extraordinary success, and generated enormous revenues.

Caught between the public clamor for tax cuts and the public's demand for continued service levels, state government officials were easily seduced by the lottery's allure. The question now is whether or not the romance of the lottery will prove to have been only an infatuation, or a "fatal attraction."

Studies suggest that the public's interest in lotteries can be fickle. Interest has been maintained, and in many instances increased, over the past seven years by the introduction of new games and more intense promotion. The level of income to the states from new programs has become so substantial that it is now impossible for any state to draw back or to ever dream of repealing its present operations.

Revenue levels automatically generate heightened expectations, and these expectations feed on themselves. And herein lies the devil's pact that policymakers make. States are caught in a vicious cycle, appropriating funds anticipated, but not yet collected, from their lotteries. If lottery income falls short of expectations the state has to "reach" to meet the projections they put in their budgets. Such reaching takes the form of new games, more outlets, and more advertising. The "bottom line" phenomenon is not restricted to the corporate boardroom. The constitutions of most states mandate balanced budgets. Nothing is uglier nor more politically damaging than to have a constitutional crisis on your hands because the budget is in deficit. No elected official can afford the stigma of irresponsibility associated with having expenditures exceed anticipated revenues. The fate of the person who underestimated the revenue is to be dispatched, with a minimum of ceremony, to political oblivion.

The pressures to increase revenue are not only persistent but also often devoid of mature reflection and measured judgment. Concepts such as regressivity, equity, and fairness must be left to those with the luxury of academic tenure, or at least the comfort of no impending election. If more dollars can be raised without requiring a new tax, it goes without question that the course of least resistance will be followed.

Indeed, revenue-raising options are always available. The proposition advanced here is that dependency on lotteries has grown to such proportions that it is presently impossible to have a serious policy debate advocating outright repeal. Rather, responsible debate must focus on suggestions for improving the present system and installing safeguards to insure that the state lotteries do not become exploitative.

Lottery revenues have had a narcotic effect on state officials. What might originally have appeared to be merely a quick fix to cope with short-term budget gaps has developed into a serious addiction. State governments are hooked badly as they watch more and more money being generated by what they would like to believe is a perpetual-motion revenue machine. Wisdom dictates that a more realistic outlook should be adopted, but that is a difficult position to advocate in light of the record of the recent past. The point of diminishing returns, however, may be around the corner. It may have already been reached by states and more mature lottery operations. Disaster is always just one scandal away. Other signals are warning states to scale back, rather than increase, revenue expectations. A weaning process must begin before lottery dependency becomes uncontrollable and irreversible.

State lotteries became big businesses very quickly, although next to the aggregate of all state taxes, which now are approximately $300 billion, lottery net receipts of $7 billion are but a fractional share. Since lotteries are not a major component of aggregated state taxes, why should we care?

First, the lottery receipts represent the fastest growing source of fresh revenue dollars to the states over the past eight years. If the federal income tax revenues had grown at the same pace as the lottery revenues, the Reagan administration would have a surplus in place of its trillion dollar deficit. Had other state revenues, such as sales taxes, paralleled the lotteries' growth, the surpluses that the various states would enjoy would prompt state legislatures to act on repeal of other existing taxes.

The second cause for concern is the sheer size to which the lotteries have grown. In gross sales, the lottery, taken as a single enterprise, ranks thirty-eighth among the *Forbes* 500, slipping in between McDonnell Douglas and BellSouth. In fact, since the results of the *Forbes* survey are based on the calendar year, and the latest available figures showing $12.8 billion for lottery sales are taken from the states' fiscal years (which ended on June 30, 1987), it is probable that lotteries actually would have moved up three or four places to challenge Xerox or Boeing.

The profits enjoyed by the combined lotteries in the United States approached the combined profits of IBM and Exxon, the number one and two profit makers of 1987. Only when added together do the profits of these two gigantic corporations exceed the net "take" that the states enjoyed from the sale of lottery tickets.

To provide a bit more perspective on the comparison of the lottery to these private enterprises, let's take a look at the asset base that is necessary in the private sector to generate the profits of the leaders. IBM had assets of almost $64 billion, and employed nearly 400,000 people, in generating its $5.2 billion in profits. Exxon had assets of $74 billion and used 101,000 employees to earn their $4.8 billion in profits. The aggregate of the state lotteries' assets can only be estimated, as is the case with the number of full-time employees from the thirty states operating lotteries. If fairness requires the most generous estimates, it would be that the state lotteries, in the aggregate, have assets and employees approaching perhaps 5 percent of the assets and employees of Exxon and IBM combined. But even with miniscule staffs and small facilities, the lotteries generate about the same amount of net profits, with the help of a network of agents working only on a commission basis.

It would be well to take a moment to dispel another common misconception not only about the lotteries, but about the gambling industry as a whole. Most people firmly believe that the casino industry bestrides the world of gambling like a colossus. The figures are misleading, because the press normally reports the "total handle," or the gross amount of money bet at the tables or in the slot machines. That figure for 1986 was almost $130 billion dollars. However, after handling and redistributing this total amount, the casino industry (consisting of an array of enterprises, from the very grand and elegant palaces on the Boardwalk in Atlantic City to the very humblest establishment in the deserts of Nevada) managed to keep less than 5 percent of the gross handle as net profit. In contrast, the lotteries, with a gross handle that amounts to only one tenth of the amount grossed by the casinos, kept almost half of the total amount handled. Tens of thousands of people owe their livelihood to the casinos. People, from the executives to the chambermaids and the busboys and everyone in between, make a living from the casino industry. The difference is startling and highlights the minimum personnel expense incurred by the lotteries. In addition to the number of jobs generated, one must also admit that the net profits are far from extraordinary and the level of taxation extracted by the two states permitting such enterprises is not confiscatory. In fact, the total of net profit and casino tax taken together is quite modest when juxtaposed next to the implied tax imposed by the lotteries.

Are these comparisons unfair? Do they lead to a distorted view? I don't think so. Lottery operations see themselves as business enterprises, not typical government agencies. Lottery officials indicate that they view their roles as business people and not as public servants.

The third important concern is taxes. Later chapters will deal extensively with this aspect. However, when viewed as a tax, which is how I think they must be viewed, one finds enormous potential for abuse of the lotteries because of their regressive nature. The abuse is not just a possibility, it is a reality. The regressivity issue is important in and by itself, but when coupled with the growth and existing size of the lottery, the public policy issues involved in the expansion and promotion of these games make it imperative that we pay much closer attention to what has been and is happening with the lotteries.

Because the states have become so heavily dependent on lottery revenue and, therefore, are unlikely to repeal the games, it is all the more critical that we undertake a serious examination. Much of the material that is presented in Part Two is not flattering to the lottery operations. The gloss of the veneer that has been put on the lotteries by professional publicists rubs off as quickly and as easily as the film covering the numbers on an instant lottery ticket. But, under the present circumstances, lottery activity is more likely to expand rather than to contract.

To demonstrate just how implausible revocation of lottery laws would be, all one need do is look at the prospects of "what if." What major taxes would have to be raised, and in what amounts, to compensate for the shortfall occasioned by the hypothetical repeal of the state's existing lottery. As an alternative, we can look at what state programs might have to be cut back or jettisoned entirely in a world without lotteries.

In New Jersey, for example, for the fiscal year 1988–1989, one might consider an across-the-board, and across-all-income classes, increase of 25 percent in the state's income tax. Alternatively, the prospect of an increase in the sales and use tax from 6 to 7 percent might be put on the table. If raising these broad-based taxes were to be considered unacceptable, as certainly they would be, then another alternative might be cutting school aid to primary and secondary schools by 16 percent, or canceling all state support for the state college system's eight institutions. Not many viable alternatives so far. There aren't any plausible or sensible options, or at least none that are attractive to those who fear the abrupt termination of their careers in public life.

While repeal may be out of the question, strong voices are being raised, some sounding only words of warning and others advocating reform. Those who have given serious thought to the options all consider it wise to adopt a more practical attitude as to what the long-range prospects are for the lotteries. A few voices are those of actual policymakers (i.e., elected officials), but it is refreshing to note that of the handful expressing concern, some are powerful and respected legislative leaders. The majority of those offering opinions contrary to the present euphoric acceptance of lottomania tend either to be academics or bureaucrats, and their warnings have smothered beneath the torrents of cash presently flowing into the states' coffers.

One such critical study was authored by John L. Mikesell and C. Kurt Zorn, professors from the University of Indiana-Bloomington. Writing in the *Public Administration Review* (July-August, 1986 issue), their article, "State Lotteries as Fiscal Savior or Fiscal Fraud: A Look at the Evidence," demonstrated the unreliability of lottery revenues: "The track record of lottery net revenues on a state-by-state basis is checkered at best. Thirteen of the 17 states which operated lotteries during the 1978-1984 period experienced decline in at least one year. These declines were as small as 0.8 percent in Massachusetts and as large as 50.0 percent in Maine." It was not just this unpredictability that concerned Mikesell and Zorn. They concluded after extensive research that "clearly, a state cannot rely on its lottery to be a stable, reliable source of net revenue. Lottery revenue is affected by changing consumer preferences, introduction of new games, marketing efforts, competition from neighboring states' games and illegal games, and other factors outside the states' control."

The state of New Jersey undertook a thorough review of its tax structure, as well as its expenditure obligations, by the State and Local Expenditure and Revenue Policy Commission. They have worked on the study since September 1985 and have invested almost $2 million on staff and on consultants' reports. A draft report on gaming revenues prepared by the staff of the Commission for review by the voting members of this blue-ribbon panel advised them that "gaming revenues have been unstable, particularly the lottery revenues. The annual percentage change of total gaming revenues, for example, ranged from 10 to 38 percent during the 1980s. They have also been cyclically sensitive. For instance, lottery sales dropped during the recession years 1973-1975."

This staff report went on to advise, "The future potential of gaming revenues is somewhat uncertain. With lotteries, the success is critically dependent on the volume of sales. Lottery sales are very volatile and the Lottery Commission faces the constant challenge of how to create and innovate and stimulate interest and sales as the lottery grows older. Increased lottery competition from neighboring states is expected to reduce state lottery sales. Game portfolios significantly affect sales and consequently revenues to the state. The Lotto has been a success and has contributed to the rapid growth in lottery sales. However, the presence of the Lotto game has hurt sales in the other games. The implication being that new games, such as Lotto, while necessary for the continued growth and stability of lottery revenues, acts as a substitute and may in themselves contribute to the decline in other games' ticket sales while adding to total lottery sales. Thus, lottery sales are expected to level off in the future." This isn't very comforting news, but one need not worry since few, if any, elected officials will pay much heed.

Elder Witt, writing in the November 1987 issue of *Governing,* warns: "Despite their growing popularity as 'painless' revenue sources, lotteries are a risky bet for states. Bettors want new games or they quit."

The author of this article also asserts, "Lotteries have a predictable life span, starting as strong revenue producers, falling off, regaining strength, and then flattening out to a slow rate of growth. Neither industry nor state officials will bet on how long a lottery can survive as a successful source of state revenues." Once again, not good news.

Mr. Witt had taken the time in preparing his story to interview Mikesell, who was still pessimistic despite the strong showing the lotteries made in 1986 and through the first six months of 1987. Mikesell was more emphatic than ever. "The danger is that we'll get confused about what a lottery is able to do and what it can't do. We'll get diverted from meaningful solutions to public problems. The lottery is not going to be the state's savior; it produces insufficient yield and unstable yield at that," he told Witt. While one can readily concur with the majority of this statement, it contains one assertion that must be questioned. How the professor defines "insufficient yield" and how governors and state legislative leaders would define that term are quite different. The difference is that the governors and legislators must get elected and reelected. So while it is truly laudable not to allow ourselves to "get diverted from meaningful solutions to public problems," it is much easier said than done. This is especially true if an election is looming.

It would be very difficult to convince the budget officers in states such as New Jersey, Pennsylvania, and Maryland, where the lotteries produce a full 5 percent of the net revenues, that the yield is "insufficient." In these states the lottery ranks fifth, fifth, and fourth, respectively, as a revenue source. Granted, it is not such a high-ranking source of revenue in such other states as New York, Illinois, Massachusetts, Ohio, Florida, Michigan, and California, but in each of these seven major states, 1988 sales will exceed the billion dollar level, and the half billion or more that this represents to their state treasuries is neither insignificant nor considered insufficient. To go back to our speculation and play "what if," we would be confronting each of these states with the uncomfortable problem of finding "meaningful solutions to public problems." Only the problem then would be not only public but also very personal to the politicians who would be forced either to cut services or to advocate major tax hikes. The lottery represents a much smaller share of overall net revenue in the balance of the New England states (excluding Massachusetts), as well as in Delaware. However, it would be difficult to find elected officials or budget officers in these states who willingly would forego their lottery revenue, or who actively would advocate raising taxes to replace the 1 to 3 percent of their state budgets that lotteries represent.

Some rare legislators in a few states have voiced opposition to, or at least concern over, the lottery operations in the states they represent. In New Jersey, the president of the Senate is an outspoken critic of the state lottery. Senator John Russo would ban advertising and maybe go as far as to phase out the lottery altogether. He is not merely concerned at what he perceives to be an increasing addiction to gambling by the public, but also by what he knows to be the state's increasing addiction to the revenues. The senator also recognizes the inherent unfairness of the present system. He is both well intentioned and powerful. Yet he also is a virtual prisoner of a system that will take more than good intentions from which to escape.

The addiction of the players and the state is acute. Administering moderate remedies is more sensible than expecting a "cold turkey" cure that would only drive the addicted players into the arms of the waiting illegal lottery operators and the addicted state treasury to a death by drowning in red ink. A scheduled and thought-out reduction of reliance on the revenues makes more sense than does repeal. Such a weaning of the state treasuries also would go a long way toward restoring a more mature and balanced attitude to the lotteries themselves. Once the hype ends we can see the games for what they are supposed to be—games. In the meantime, lotteries are here to stay. Optimistically, the good intentions of leaders such as John Russo can be directed toward the reforms that, if implemented, could vastly improve the lottery systems not only in his state, but in other states as well.

PART II

4

Lotteries as State Tax Policy

A quorum call in either house of the New Jersey Legislature on the day of an important tax vote is always certain to bring out erratic behavior in men and women, who, under less stressful circumstances, normally comport themselves responsibly and decorously. As majority leader and then as speaker, I recall more than a few occasions when I was forced to search for and ferret out members of the Assembly who had retreated to their favorite nooks and crannies in the cavernous State House, hoping to escape detection before the dreaded tax measure was called for a vote. Over the years, colleagues serving as leaders in other states have told me that my experience was far from unique.

Taxes of any description are not high on any legislator's list of favorite agenda items, and tax alternatives, such as a lottery, are easily viewed as some type of panacea. With their backs to the wall, legislators demonstrate a distinct preference for those measures least likely to incite heavy political reaction. Revenue-raising proposals that avoid easy identification as taxes—"surcharges" for example—are much in style; and the more artfully hidden, the better, when it comes to taxes. Some levies are hidden so well that it is difficult to see on whom the burden actually falls, but it is even more common to see legislatures resort to the expedient of adopting measures admitted to be regressive, and lotteries are what many consider to be the most regressive of all forms of taxation.

Regressive tax policy is most easily diagnosed by the absence of vertical equity, that function of a state's tax system which spreads the burden across income classes equally on the basis of each class's ability to pay. Vertical equity is basically a barometer of how much of one's disposable income is consumed by support of the government, from the state house to the schoolhouse.

Here is a simple example: One family earns $100,000 and pays a total of $10,000 in state and local taxes, or 10 percent of its income. If another family earns only $20,000 and is taxed the same 10 percent (or $2,000), such a system is said to have vertical equity.

If, however, the higher-earning family pays only $5,000, or 5 percent of its disposable income in state and local taxes, while the lower-income family pays $3,000, or 15 percent of its disposable income, the system is regressive.

The figures used in this example are close to the actual rates in effect throughout the country. In 1987, the national average of state-local taxes per $100 of personal income was $11.35, according to the National Conference of State Legislatures. The lowest state on the scale was New Hampshire, collecting only $8.48 per $100 of income. Wyoming and Alaska were on the high end of the scale, with apparent rates of more than $17.00. Data from these two states unfairly skews the average, however, because both states receive the lion's share of their revenue from taxes on oil production and a very small amount is actually paid by the ordinary citizen. Forty of the fifty states fall in the $9.50 to $12.00 range. Remember, the important figures for this investigation involve not the overall averages, but rather the averages for the various income ranges.

Most state and local taxes, such as sales, use, excise, property and utility taxes, tend to be regressive. It is not uncommon to see wage earners in the low-income brackets being forced to pay 20 percent (or even more) of their incomes for these taxes, while high-income earners pay only 5 or 6 percent. Fair share levies, or vertical equities, are absent from the system.

Just as an entire tax structure can lack vertical equity, we can judge the vertical equity to be found in individual taxes by the way they operate. The gas tax is a good example. It is levied without discrimination. The rich and the poor pay the same amount every time they buy fuel for their cars. As a percentage of disposable income, gas taxes fall more heavily on the poor. They do, however, possess what is called "horizontal equity" in that everyone is taxed at the same flat rate. No discount is provided for large-volume users, and there is no income level or minimum usage level that exempts anyone from paying.

Income taxes are commonly held to come closest to attaining the progressive ideal. Escalating rates with exemptions at the lower end of the income scale create situations that accurately reflect a person's ability to pay, and, therefore, such taxes may be considered progressive.

Lottery spokespersons seldom, if ever, refer to the lottery as a tax. In lottery parlance, euphemisms such as "take-out" describe revenues generated by lotteries. You may find a rare lottery official willing to describe the lottery as a voluntary tax, or, sometimes, a "tax alternative."

Lottery advocates have devised other euphemisms to shield the playing public from realizing that they are being taxed. Ticket buyers are always referred to as "players," never as taxpayers. There is a certain romance in being referred to as a "player"; a certain panache is associated with the word. It conjures up glamorous images of striped awnings over the clubhouse veranda at the race track or tuxedoed dealers passing the shoe at a baccarat table. There is nothing romantic or glamorous about being just another statistic—faceless and anonymous—a mere taxpayer. The idea is to lead the public to believe that unlike a taxpayer who faces only the inevitable, a player has limitless opportunities spread out before him.

Who are these players? Various and fine independent studies by scholars and lottery commissions provide some interesting answers to this question. Whether analyzed by state agencies, scholars, or marketing companies, the findings lead to one inescapable conclusion: Lotteries are driven by the poor and the undereducated.

In Canada, a former Provincial official spoke frankly about who the players are, and what type of tax is being levied on them. David Barrett served as Premier of British Columbia from 1972 to 1976. During his tenure, a lottery was initiated. In retrospect, Barrett considers its adoption a mistake. "It's simply a regressive and unfair form of taxation that lower-income people pay. We hadn't intended it that way, but that is the way it has worked out. The poor are the biggest buyers, and the wealthy rarely, if ever, participate at all.

A Maryland study sheds more light on the market and consequent marketing tactics that make lotteries prosperous. It compared two market areas, Baltimore City and Montgomery County, the poorest and the wealthiest markets, respectively, in the state of Maryland. At the time of the study, Baltimore City had a population of 764,000, or about 18 percent of the state's residents. Median household income was $16,829, with almost 50 percent of all households having incomes less than $25,000, and only 3.1 percent having an income greater than $50,000. Contrast this with Montgomery County, with a population of 589,000, or 14 percent of the entire state. The median household income was almost double that of Baltimore City's at $33,676, and only 6 percent had incomes less than $15,000 while 22 percent had incomes greater than $50,000.

Baltimore City had 396 outlet terminals (or 32 percent of the state's total), while only 101 terminals (or 8 percent of the state's outlets) could be found in affluent Montgomery County. Of all "Pick 3" sales, 33 percent were in Baltimore City, with 8 percent in Montgomery County. "Pick 4" numbers paralleled those of the other game; 28 percent of these sales took place in Baltimore City, and 9.7 percent were sold in Montgomery.

New Jersey conducted an extensive study of its own. The results were made public in the summer of 1988. The study cost the state over a quarter of a million dollars, and it was hoped that it would enjoy widespread credibility. The report, prepared by Allison Jackson Associates and Response Analysis Corporation of Princeton, was greeted with extraordinary skepticism. While acknowledging that the lottery was regressive, because it was played more heavily by blacks, Hispanics, and the poor, the report concluded that the game was only slightly regressive. In addition, the report concluded that since it wasn't perceived to be exploitative, the lottery, in fact, wasn't. What this report lacked in logic, common sense, and accuracy, it made up for in statistics. Sadly, many of these were so grossly incorrect that the original benign skepticism quickly turned to ridicule. Finally, when the compilers of the study admitted that they discarded data that indicated extreme regressivity and exploitation, the majority of the report's conclusions were called into very serious question.

Try as they might, the 1988 findings of regressivity could not be hidden, and they only confirmed similar findings from previous studies. In fact, this study did not even inquire into the most relevant area; no information was given regarding the percentage of the total annual sales that could be attributable to the number of tickets purchased by the poor. In other words, we can not ascertain from this expensive study whether or not the poor are buying only 20 percent of the tickets or are they buying 40 percent of the total tickets sold. A poll taken in 1986 by the *Newark Star-Ledger,* in conjunction with the Eagleton Institute of Politics at Rutgers, the State University of New Jersey, showed that of those New Jerseyans who bought tickets at least once a week, 44 percent earned between $15,000 and $30,000. It further indicated that 35 percent earned more than $30,000 a year. Moreover, 46 percent had high school educations or better. We may conclude, therefore, that 21 percent of the ticket buyers had incomes of less than $15,000 a year. Assuming these figures to hold for 1988, when the state expects over a billion dollars in sales, it converts more than $210 million of ticket sales being made to those on the edge of, or below, the poverty line.

The state will keep at least $100 million from those sales as its "take out," or tax. That will be $100 million dollars taken knowingly from the poorest of the poor. Second, it would show that 54 percent of the players don't have a basic high school diploma. Clearly, this is not something that the state marketers of a lottery system should want to brag about.

A survey conducted by the New Jersey Lottery in 1985 differed from the Eagleton Institute's findings, which had indicated that 21 percent of the players had incomes below $15,000 per year. The Lottery Commission's 1988 survey found only 15 percent of the players to have incomes that low. Once again, given sales at the billion dollar level, extracting "only" $150 million in gambling money from the very poor should give scant comfort to the formulators of public policy.

Findings of the Maryland study were submitted to the U.S. Senate and included in the Subcommittee on Intergovernmental Relations' final report in 1984. The study compared the demographics of Maryland and New Jersey to suggest that if one type of game sold well to a specific segment of the New Jersey population, then predictably it would sell well to a similar segment of the Maryland population. The study said it was that "in any given lottery game, if a group from New Jersey participates to a high degree, this may be indicative of the degree of participation to the same demographic group in Maryland. This view is supported by a *Public Gaming* magazine study of six other state lotteries, where the overall results were basically the same." In considering this data, it is helpful to know that an index number of 100 for a particular group and game means that the particular group participates in a game at a rate equal to that group's presence in the population. Numbers higher than 100 indicate that a given group plays more heavily; conversely, numbers below 100 indicate less participation. The study uses 1980 dollar figures.

New Jersey residents with incomes of over $56,000 amounted to 6.1 percent of the population. On the other end of the spectrum are the 12.2 percent of the population with annual incomes under $6,700. For the "Pick 3" game, the participation index for the wealthiest group was 71, but for the poorest group, the index shot up to 125. In the "Pick 4" game, the index for those in the highest income category rose to 75, and the participation by the poorest dropped to 109. The data also examine sales by gender. New Jersey's population breaks down to 48 percent male and 52 percent female. On "Pick 3," male participation was 116, while the female index was only 83. This division of participation held true even on the "Pick 6" lotto game. The education breakdowns are also very instructive. New Jerseyans with four years of college or more constituted 11.8 percent of the population, while 28 percent of the state had only eighth grade or less. Those with a college degree or higher registered an index of 79 for the "Pick 3," while those with an elementary education or less scored a 115.

Having seen a systematic cross-section of the lottery-buying public, it would be instructive to look at a study conducted by those seeking to expand the gaming market.

John R. Koza, head of Scientific Games, one of the leading suppliers to the lottery industry, wrote a four-part series for *Public Gaming* magazine. The series was entitled, "Who is Playing What," and recounted what various market groups liked to spend their money on when it came to forms of games of chance. Lotteries were only one of thirty-two gambling activities that ranged from bingo to horse racing. The highest lottery participation was an index rating of 189.2, which applied to lower-middle-income classes of Eastern European heritage living in the northeastern United States. This was followed by an index rating of 164, found in older rental housing occupied by blacks. Down in fifth place on the index scale, but still high at 120, are poor families living in very deteriorated housing in Hispanic neighborhoods. These findings showing that lotteries are driven by the poor and disadvantaged are paralleled in other studies as well.

In November 1987, Elder Witt summarized some of these classic studies in *Governing* magazine: "For example, studies of lottery participants show that people with less money tend to play the numbers games in which a three or four digit number is bet on and picked each day. But lotto, in which the player tries to choose the winning combination of six numbers, attracts far more bettors with more money, including a substantial portion of people who live in the suburbs.

"Blacks tend to spend $4.50 per week more to play the Maryland lottery than do whites," concluded Charles T. Clotfelder and Philip J. Cook of Duke University, after studying participation in that state's lottery. They found that the less education a person has, the more enthusiastically he tends to play the lottery. White high-school dropouts spend an average of $5 more per week on the lottery than do white college graduates. The elderly spend the least on the lottery, the Clotfelder–Cook study reported, and persons between the ages of 25 to 54 spend the most. The study also showed that "males spend more than females: white males spend about $1 per week more than white females, and black males spend about $4 per week more than black females."

The Los Angeles *Times* also conducted a study in the spring of 1986, which found that the weekly expenditure on instant game tickets in California was 2.1 percent of household income in households whose incomes were below $10,000 per year. This rate dropped on a straight graph line until it was shown that in the above $60,000 per year income range, weekly expenditure on instant game tickets was only 0.3 percent of household income. What this all means is that a family earning $10,000 spent $210 a year on lottery tickets, while a family with an annual income six times higher spent only $180 a year. With these figures in front of them, Clotfelder and Cook had no problem, nor should anyone else, in describing this pattern as clearly regressive.

Lottery boosters still insist that the participation is broad, but the numbers are against them. Their answers are claims of voluntariness and their distaste for paternalism. Mikesell and Zorn, after reviewing all of the literature, put it simply in a 1986 article: "Public finance scholars...employ the standard analysis of vertical equity and conclude that state lotteries place a greater relative burden on low-income families than on high-income families and that use of state lotteries reduces the net income of low-income groups relative to that of high-income groups. This regressivity of state lotteries has been demonstrated frequently and decisively. The pattern is strong, even leading to the conclusion that, by some measures, lottery regressivity is double that of a state sales tax. From the position of government finance, there is no doubt that state lotteries violate the standard of vertical equity."

The state of New Jersey completed a comprehensive tax and spending study in April 1988. After extensively reviewing gaming revenues in the state, the final report contains this one-sentence conclusion: "Incidence of gaming revenues is found to be regressive, particularly in the incidence of lottery revenues."

It is clear that lotteries are regressive. A comparative judgment will show just how regressive they really are.

The allegedly most regressive taxes, the sales and use taxes, vary from state to state. The highest is the tax imposed by Connecticut, at a rate of 7.5 percent, on most items including all adults' clothing, beer, wine, and liquor for on-and-off-premises consumption, and cigarettes. Potentially, New York state's sales tax can even go higher, with the state getting 4 percent and the counties and municipalities authorized to tack on another 4 percent. New York, by the way, only excludes food bought for off-premises consumption, places its tax on all clothing, and even levies it against motor fuel sales. Maryland taxes sales at 5 percent, including alcohol by the drink, as well as all clothing. Many states, in an attempt to ameliorate the regressivity of the general sales tax, have exempted many items considered to be staples or necessities, leaving the tax to fall only on discretionary purchases. The rate can likewise be expressed in terms of an effective rate. This term tells us generally how much of a person's disposable income goes to sales taxes in a given state after the exemptions are factored in. New Jersey exempts all clothing and all food items bought at the supermarket. This is considered to be as liberal as any state is with its sales tax. The result is that the effective rate is about 4 percent for the low-income group and only 2 percent for the wealthiest group. We can talk about the rates themselves or we can consider the effective rates. For our present purposes it makes little difference.

The take-out rate or implied tax of the lotteries is not 5 or even 7 percent. It is closer to 50 percent. No matter how you view it, the lottery is about ten times higher than the general sales tax rate in effect in the majority of the states. Of course, this basic take-out rate or implied tax is an aggregate tax, since not all, but only most, of the players lose. To make this a bit more graphic, assume a million-dollar jackpot based on two million separate people buying one ticket each. The state keeps one million dollars as take-out and pays one million dollars to one individual. What was the effective tax rate on the 1,999,999 people who lost? It is clear that for that particular drawing the rate on those losers was actually 100 percent. However, since there was one person who won, the aggregate implied tax was only 50 percent.

Take all the drawings into account and of course the aggregate take-out will always be in the 50 percent range. For the poor soul who has never won, the tax rate remains at 100 percent. And what about the person in our hypothetical drawing who actually hit the jackpot? In some states, the winnings would be exempt from any state income tax, but they would not be exempt from the federal income tax which presumably would be levied at the maximum rate of 28 percent. After paying the Internal Revenue Service, a good portion of the net winnings will be spent on items that in most states will be subject to sales tax. Of the original two million dollars put up in the betting pool, it is reasonable to project that over 85 percent of it, or $1.7 million will find its way into the coffers of either the state or federal government.

When it comes to large jackpots it is extremely rare for a state to make anything more than an annual payment. A million-dollar jackpot winner normally wins $50,000 per year, for twenty years. Advertising for such games often includes some notification, in small print, that the jackpot is actually only an "annuity," or something to that effect. This would be considered fair if it were not for the fact that only one person in twenty has even the remotest idea of what an annuity is. The 1988 New Jersey study, referred to earlier, indicated that there were actually people who didn't realize that the large prizes weren't paid in lump sums. Even more surprising was the assertion that the majority of those interviewed preferred annual installments to lump-sum payments. There are those who would suggest that this alone constituted sufficient reason to ban lotteries, as people obviously aren't smart enough to be allowed to play them.

At one time, there was some justification for this procedure. The states operating lotteries prior to 1981 originally defended this pay-out method as being fairer to the winners. This argument was reasonable at a time when federal tax rates were set at levels that might have exposed a lump-sum payment to confiscatory rates. However, when top tax rates were lowered, the states' justification for these annuity payments disappeared. It is regrettable that as top federal tax rates lowered, so did the level of the states' solicitude for its lottery winners.

Under the Tax Reform Act of 1986, it now makes very little, if any, difference to the winner from a federal tax perspective, whether the money is paid in a lump-sum or in annual installments. It does make an enormous difference to the states, a very positive difference. For the winners, the difference between a lump-sum payment and an annuity is extremely negative, now that federal tax treatment has become irrelevant. Lottery winners lose even when they win.

Assume once again that $2 million dollars are wagered in order to create an alleged million-dollar jackpot. The state, instead of paying out the million dollars, must only make installment payments of fifty thousand per year. That is less than the interest the state will make on the million dollars each year. If the winner were to receive the actual jackpot, steps could be taken by the winner to protect their winnings from further tax obligations by investment in exempt bonds. The net annual yield at current rates would be higher than what they now get under the annuity system. More important, at the end of the twenty years, the winner would have the redemption value of the bonds. Under the present pay-out scheme, all they have is their memories of having once thought they were rich. Moreover, the effect of inflation is never mentioned by the states as they schedule the high-profile events that have become part of the expected ritual in handing out the first installment check to the jackpot winners. The winner of an alleged million dollar jackpot may feel wealthy today, but it is a good bet that $50,000, less federal tax, will not have a great deal of purchasing power in the year 2008. In that year the state, which had introduced the winner to the press with such fanfare back in 1988, will still have the million dollars— plus all the extra interest they had made on the winner's money over the course of 20 years.

In actuality, the state will not have the same million dollars. The state buys an annuity for the winner. The cost of an annuity that will pay its owner $50,000 per year for the next twenty years was, in the spring of 1988, less than $500,000. The winning player prevailed over odds that were indeed one in a million, yet the real value of his win is substantially less than what the odds warranted. This annual payment method lost its justification years ago, but the cynicism that pervades the lottery system continues to triumph, and again, it is a matter of what the market will bear.

The federal taxation of lottery winnings is a price most winners are still happy to pay. The players are also apparently also willing, whether they win or lose, to bear the highest excise tax imposed on any lawful activity. A special index for measuring the equivalent rate of excise taxation for state lotteries was developed by Roger E. Brinner together with Professor Clotfelder in 1975. It first appeared in an article they coauthored for the *National Tax Journal* entitled "An Economic Appraisal of State Lotteries." According to this method of comparison, which has never been challenged, the national average excise rate on the state lotteries was 64 percent, with a high rate of 91 percent in New York and a low rate of 35 percent in Vermont.

Daniel B. Suits was among the first to demonstrate the regressive nature of the lottery systems. His was the unenviable role of being a relatively lone voice trying to argue the facts, while legions of professional publicists were deluging the public with misleading data and denigrating anyone such as Suits, who had the temerity to mention that the systems were overtaxing the poor.

Defenders of the existing lottery systems generally respond to regressivity concerns by challenging the very idea that the lottery is a tax. Maryland Lottery Director Martin M. Puncke echoes many of his fellow lottery directors when he contends that lotteries are an entertainment fee, or "user fee" similar to the fee charged for admission to a state park or beach.

Another comparison used to debunk the notion of the lottery as a tax is to make it akin to the fees paid to a state-run liquor store for the purchase of alcohol. Entertainment is purchased and no tax is actually extracted, according to this argument. Lottery sales must then be considered just another item in the inventory of government products that are for sale exclusively by the sovereign or its subdivisions. Even for budget and audit purposes these revenues must appear as other income since it is really not a tax, but more in the nature of a voluntary fee paid only if the person chooses to use the service or product being made available to them by the state.

Some will undoubtedly find such responses persuasive, if only superficially. What these semantic niceties cannot hide is the fact that user fees fundamentally are also regressive, and often highly so. Liquor taxes, or the fees paid when the purchase is directly from a state store, are probably the most regressive of all standard taxes. As to the user fees charged for use of parks and beaches, they rarely, if ever, are enough to compensate for the costs of the operation and maintenance of facilities. In fact, heavy subsidization from general revenues is customary for the normal and traditional recreational opportunities provided by the government, other than the lottery.

Ultimately, it makes no difference what label we use. It is the lottery's effect that must be considered. Whether we say the lottery is a tax, a tax equivalent, an implied tax, an excise tax, a sin tax, a voluntary tax, or even a nontax; whether we think of it as fee, a user fee, or even an entertainment fee, the reality of the facts do not change—four of every five dollars bet find their way rapidly into the treasuries of either the state or federal government. Compounding the problem is that dollars gambled do not come from the pockets of the wealthy, but from the middle class and the poor, and, in a disturbing proportion, from the very poor. The states have been hard pressed to find additional and new sources of revenue, but not so hard pressed as to justify the institutionalization of avarice that is reflected in the present regressivity of the state-operated lotteries.

A total cure for the regressivity of the lotteries may not be possible. But that should not dissuade anyone from giving serious consideration to suggestions addressed to reducing their regressivity and ameliorating some of their most obnoxious qualities. Three recommendations to do just that are spelled out in the chapter on tax reform.

5

State Lotteries: Grafting Private Enterprise onto Government Structures

A strong theme running consistently through our history has been that the role of the sovereign is to govern, not to participate in private enterprise. Rarely, if ever, does a state go into a business, although it is not unheard of for a state to find itself in an enterprise that normally would be left to the private sector. In these rare instances where we find a state engaged in a proprietary function it is usually the result of the private sector's failure to satisfactorily fill a definite public need. Some well-known examples are the Tennessee Valley Authority and state-run mass transit systems. More often, a state is found operating an activity that is considered to be so questionable or vulnerable to abuse that it cannot be entrusted to private interests. After prohibition, for example, the sale of alcohol was considered to be so morally delicate a matter that many states took on the responsibility of selling alcohol by having state-run liquor stores.

Lotteries are not quite like anything else that exists within the traditional framework of state governments; not even state-operated liquor concessions. Therefore, it is warranted that these state-operated lotteries be examined from a public-policy perspective. These games of chance, which are now run by twenty-nine states, constitute a unique phenomenon. They are held out to be just another square on the organization charts of the state governments, and allegedly are designed to be vaguely "regulatory" in nature. But, in practice, they have but one goal, and that is to sell tickets and bring in as many dollars as possible.

Has this resulted in a split personality? Not at all. The state-run lotteries have a perfect understanding of what they are and what they are not. More importantly, they know exactly what they are supposed to do, and how to do it—make money.

Given this, what deserves the most careful examination is the problem of the double standard that has insinuated itself into both the general perception of the lotteries and into the way they conduct their business. Practices that would be considered deviant and objectionable in the private sector are tacitly approved, while the criteria used for the operations of other divisions of government are considered not to apply to this anomalous state operation. While we clamor for truth in advertising, and insist that every consumer be provided with detailed information before borrowing even a small amount of money, lotteries are permitted to operate in an environment free from scrutiny. While government interjects itself to prescribe what constitutes the elements of a citizen's right to know as it applies to everything—from the chemicals being manufactured in the local factory, down to the milligrams of sodium in the can of soup you serve for lunch—lotteries function in a world virtually free of restraint. The situation is such that lotteries are usually immune from criticism, and are normally praised for the enormous amounts of monies that they generate for the states. This double standard is not merely some historical quirk. Rather, it is at the core of the entire process of state-operated gambling. Tolerance of this double standard fosters hypocrisy as official public policy, inspires a mounting cynicism in those who give even the most cursory study to these operations and discover where a good deal of the revenue is coming from.

It was recently reported in a national magazine that in 1987 only one of California's 21,000 lottery agents had been disciplined for selling a ticket to a minor. The offending agent had his license to sell tickets suspended for thirty days. Can you recall any other instance that you've read or even heard about involving a report of a crackdown by the authorities on an agent for selling state lottery tickets to someone underage or under the influence of alcohol? That is not to say that enforcement actions don't take place, but only that they result in very little, if any, publicity. The normal standard is that a true regulatory agency seeks as much attention as possible when a disciplinary action is undertaken to deter other would-be transgressors.

For reasons best known only to the states themselves, offenses such as improper inducements and questionable promotions go totally unreported and undiscussed. Revocations and cancellations of the license to sell lottery tickets for the states have occurred; but they usually are because of an insufficient volume of sales, not dereliction of duty or fraud. Not selling enough tickets is a serious matter, requiring quick and decisive action. Having a state agency impose penalties for failure to sell a quota on the one hand, while ignoring traditional licensing infractions on the other, is the most blatant example of the double standard in operation.

It has come to the point where the states no longer engage in the pretense that their lottery operations have any obligation for meaningful regulation, only for increased sales and tax revenue.

The present situation leads to a number of important questions that should be answered. To begin with, who is regulating the lottery systems, and what kind of public policy is reflected in a system that allows hucksterism to masquerade in the cloak of an agency often labeled as "regulatory"? Haven't we created for ourselves a substantial and inherent conflict of interest by the way we designed the lottery operations in state after state? Finally, aren't we tolerating a double standard that has been elevated to the status of public policy?

Perhaps the best way to pursue these inquiries is to first look at a bona fide regulatory agency, and then look at some typical state agencies that are unabashedly promotional in nature. Next, we examine what some state lottery directors, as well as others involved in lottery operations, have actually said about how they perceive their roles. Finally, we undertake the analysis that is required to assess exactly what type of vacuum exists as a result of how selling tickets engages the entire time, effort, energy, and attention of the state officials running the lotteries, leaving little room for active enforcement or regulation, and apparently no time for reflection on how the systems could be improved.

Only two states presently have casino gaming, Nevada and New Jersey. To give you some idea of how seriously New Jersey takes its responsibility of properly regulating casinos, compare the following statistics. In 1986, the eleven casinos licensed to do business in the state paid a total of $181.2 million to the state under the casino tax. In order to paint the best possible picture of this enterprise, we should include all other assorted tax revenues generated for the state by the casinos. So, let's add monies paid in the form of the corporate business tax, state unemployment taxes, liquor taxes, luxury taxes, employee income taxes, sales and use taxes, and even the special reinvestment obligation that the state wrote into its Casino Act. Calculating all of these revenues, they indicate that the state collected just under $300 million in all taxes associated with the operation of legalized casino gambling in that year. (This figure does not include the $44 million in "regulatory fees" which support the Casino Control Commission and the Division of Gaming Enforcement.)

On the other hand, net income to the state from the lottery in this same year was $418 million, or almost 30 percent more than what was raised for the state by the whole casino industry. Of the $418 million that was collected by the state as their take-out from lottery sales, an amount that could only fairly be described as miniscule went for control or enforcement of any kind, or at least what we commonly think of as enforcement.

The New Jersey Casino Control Commission consists of five full-time commissioners who are paid respectable salaries for the job they do, which is to oversee not only the licensing of the casinos, but literally every aspect of casino operations. In New Jersey, the control of casino activities is considered to be so important that the commissioners receive salaries higher than the salary of the governor. The Division of Gaming Enforcement is housed within the attorney general's office and has 580 employees, all of whom are there to keep an eye on the day-to-day, night-to-night, and hour-by-hour operations of the eleven casinos.

New Jersey's Lottery Commission, in contrast, consists of seven members serving part time, which means that they attend monthly meetings. They are paid $3,500 year. There is, of course, an executive director who is paid a cabinet-level salary for a full-time position. As far as can be discerned from public records, the lottery office has no employees assigned exclusively to enforcement or investigation. There is a deputy director who is in charge of "security," but he is also responsible for auditing and licensing, and it has been impossible to find out precisely if anyone in this section does any investigating beyond the standard reviews of applications for franchising permits.

The standards for casino gambling are dramatically different. The Division of Gaming Enforcement critically reviews over 20,000 applications a year. Everyone and everything associated with the casino industry is checked and rechecked. In addition, this division regularly audits the accounts of every casino. Any alleged impropriety is thoroughly investigated. One would love to think that, during 1987, not even one of the 4,200 lottery agents sold a ticket to a minor or someone inebriated, nor had any agent played loan shark to an addicted customer or paid someone a gratuity for generating new customers for their outlet. The number of disciplinary actions taken by the New Jersey Lottery Commission during 1987 was insignificant.

The state, while priding itself on the strict level of scrutiny it maintains in the casinos, turns an absolute blind eye toward the operations of the lottery.

Not all agencies of a state are designed to engage in investigations, regulation, enforcement, or control of any kind. Every state has some agencies whose mission it is to indirectly generate tax dollars by promoting a specific area of the state's economy, or to encourage the overall prosperity of the state. For purposes of comparison and analysis we can examine some typical ones.

No state is without an Office of Economic Development or something similar. They are set up to encourage new businesses, and to facilitate any enterprise that is looking for a potential site for new or relocating plants. These offices keep centralized files of available properties, information on the ease of providing roads and utilities, long lists of the attributes of the state, and are, in effect, the chambers of commerce with the states' seals on their office doors.

It is not uncommon for these agencies of the states to have advertising budgets. However, when we speak of the states' investing in self-promotion, the type of agency that comes to mind immediately is the standard state office of tourism. New York, Florida, California, and Virginia waged such successful campaigns in the early years of this decade that many other states aggressively joined in with splashy and often very attractive efforts of their own to promote the appeal of their facilities as a vacation destination. Television is the preferred medium, with radio also widely used. The latest innovation is the broadcasting of these state tourist ads in Europe.

No criticism of these agencies or their practices is intended. These examples are offered to demonstrate the difference between the structures and methods states use when they are in a true regulatory mode, as is the case of overseeing the casinos, and when they are in a boosterism mode, as in the case with tourism promotion. The activities of these economic development and tourism promotion boards and their advertising is normally generic. The message is neither product or site specific. In this respect, they differ enormously from the state-run lotteries, which, of course concentrate their large advertising efforts on a specific product. They do not differ, however, in how they view their roles within the states' scheme of things.

Before arriving at even an interim judgment as to where we should place state lottery operations within the framework of traditional government structures, we should look at exactly how the lottery operators view themselves. The evidence is in the form of the statements of the commission directors, others involved in the running of the lotteries, and knowledgeable observers. Oregon started its lottery in 1985. The first director of their operation, Robert Smith, stated in a moment of refreshing candor that running a lottery is "a competitive, specialized entertainment business." How did he view his role? "It is not a regulatory agency. We were promoting the game, not trying to control it," he said bluntly in the November 1987 issue of *Governing* magazine. This attitude didn't change much by March 1988, when Steven Caputo, the deputy director of the Oregon lottery, was interviewed by *State Government News,* a magazine published by the Council of State Governments. Caputo said, "You have to approach it as business. If expectations are to have the lottery as a viable revenue raiser, you must give it the tools...to advertise and market a product."

Barbara Marrow, director of the New Jersey lottery, had the following to say about her role to the Newark *Star-Ledger,* the state's largest newspaper, in November 1987: "Who are we to say to that person that they can't have leisure in their life, that every penny should go to food, clothing, and shelter? I'm not saying people who receive public assistance should play the lottery, but I can't encourage them not to." The article goes on to say that Director Marrow added that it was the state law that made it *her duty to run an efficient lottery.* The italics are added for emphasis, but perhaps it isn't needed. The point should be clear that those in charge of the lotteries see their duties in very narrow terms. It is only a business. Moreover, it is a business that government is not accustomed to operating. Consider the following statement by the public information officer for the Iowa lottery, Jack Ratekin: "This is something that people in government are not used to doing. We hired marketing professionals and it paid off."

Perhaps the most telling comment comes from a statement made by Terri LaFluer, who writes a column for the magazine *Gaming and Wagering Business*. (It is virtually impossible to read any article about lotteries without finding some words of insight from the knowledgeable and well-informed Ms. LaFluer.) In *Governing* magazine she says, "A lottery agency is different from any other agency in state government. They run a business. It's not easy to graft a profit-raising organ on a structure that basically spends money, instead of raising it." This statement says a great deal; in fact, it goes directly to the heart of the issue. Government is designed to govern, and that takes money. Traditionally, those funds are raised by taxation, not by adopting a profit-oriented enterprise. Indeed, grafted-on material doesn't always fit perfectly. In the case of lotteries, the host structure hasn't cared much about how the graft looks, but only how well it has produced revenues.

Elaine S. Knapp, senior editor of *State Government News,* concluded: "Successful state lotteries are run as businesses, with minimal state restrictions."

All of the enabling acts and referenda that put lotteries into operation throughout this country and in Canada over the past twenty years contain one word: integrity. Every state and province says that it wants to have an operation which insures the integrity of the system. In fairness, it is possible to place a very narrow definition on the term "integrity." However, it is also fair to assume that the drafters of the various pieces of legislation had something more in mind than that the governor's family would not know the number before it was drawn.

State lottery operations appear to have opted for the narrowest of definitions of integrity, and have chosen to view their roles solely as that of revenue generators without even a modicum of responsibility for regulation of their agents or themselves. Less restraint and fewer restrictions seem to be the order of the day as more and more states get caught up in the present wave of lottomania.

Let us go back once again to the simple question of who is charged with the obligation of seeing to it that these games of chance are conducted and regulated in a fashion that instills confidence by their fairness and forthrightness. We must conclude that the states either do not see this as their responsibility, or worse, choose not to do anything that might have a chilling or inhibiting effect on the level of participation. After all, it's not good policy to revoke the license of agents who are big-volume sellers. In fact, it is more than that: It is impossible to expect a state agency whose real and only duty is to raise revenue to do anything at all that would be counterproductive to that money-making goal. Innate and inherent conflict exists, and will, of necessity, continue to exist, as long as lottery operators view their mandate as one that is limited to running a smooth, efficient, and, above all else, profitable operation.

The structural conflict built into lottery operations leads inevitably to problems. Failure to adequately or meaningfully regulate their agents is indeed a minor problem when compared to the states' failure, refusal, or inability to regulate and control themselves. The problem of one agent selling a ticket to a juvenile is rather insignificant compared to the policy decision to put more outlets into areas demographically known to be poor. An agent pushing extra purchases on a drunk pales in comparison to a state's decision to adopt an advertising theme that pushes more tickets on an entire class or ethnic group of low-income people. An agent advancing a small loan to a steady customer isn't very serious when compared to the policy decision to rely more heavily on a regressive tax.

So we are really back to the basic question of who will regulate the regulators. Who is going to really ensure the integrity of the system? A system that is abusive in its promotional techniques, and exploitative in its advertising campaigns, is devoid of integrity. Simply put, a system that systematically milks the poor doesn't have integrity.

Three ways to ensure integrity are as follows:

1. Regulations of distribution outlets to ensure that poor areas are not oversaturated;
2. Regulation of advertising campaigns to ensure that they are honest and not exploitative; and
3. Regulation of state tax policies to ensure that they are not regressive.

State lottery operations as presently constituted are not providing, nor are they capable of providing, these safeguards. Indeed, as long as increased sales and the subsequent additional revenue are their only businesses, lotteries must move inexorably toward more outlets and more aggressive advertising to generate a tax whose impact is increasingly regressive.

The following chapters examine how lotteries, through marketing, advertising, and revenue raising, have become an integral part of many state governments. This analysis suggests a fundamental restructuring is in order—a restructuring that will divorce operational functions from regulatory functions, and restore public policy to a more traditional and reasoned standard.

6

Marketing the Lotteries: Present Practices

State-run lotteries, then, are bound by competing interests. They cannot regulate themselves or their agents without running the serious risk of dampening the betting action. The last chapter established that the problem results from an absence of adequate regulation of lotteries as state-run, profit-oriented, commercial enterprises, grafted uncomfortably onto the traditional structure of government.

In this chapter, we focus more narrowly on one specific anomaly of the present administrative functioning of the state lotteries, and how that anomaly exacerbates harmful marketing practices that only make state-run lotteries more exploitative. This anomaly is the consequence of lotteries' unique status as state-operated gambling monopolies.

Monopolies have been held in disfavor in every free society. In the United States, antipathy toward monopolies is reflected by state and federal antitrust laws. Yet, as a practical matter, we tolerate regulated monopolies such as public utilities. We understand that it would be wasteful and inefficient to have two separate electric, gas, or water companies.

When we think of state-granted monopolies we think most often of typical public utilities. But there is a second type of enterprise whose activities are considered either so essential to the public welfare, or so potentially harmful that state governments have imposed strong regulations on them through licensing.

Banking and health care are two enterprises whose existence is essential to the public welfare, and as such, are heavily regulated. The distribution and sale of alcohol, and the conduct of games of chance, are businesses considered so inherently vulnerable to abuse that they must be heavily regulated.

These second-tier enterprises are quasi-monopolies or oligopolies in their structure and function. Casino gambling in New Jersey and Nevada is the quintessential oligopoly. State-run lotteries are not quasi-anything. They are classic state monopolies that would do credit to the mercantile economic philosophy of the court of Louis XIV.

The concept of "public convenience" is used by the government to provide due process to various competing applicants for certain special privileges. It is applied to all private monopolies and quasi-monopolies, such as banks, hospitals, and liquor stores, to determine who shall be licensed or franchised. In the law, "convenience" is not used in its colloquial sense, but is defined as "suitable and fitting." To satisfy the statutory requirement of convenience the regulated enterprise must be appropriate and suited to fulfill a legitimate public need.

Adherence to the concept of public convenience normally involves demonstrating that the population of the jurisdiction warrants the issuance of the license. Typical regulations provide for one liquor license to be issued for every 5,000 in population. Applicants normally also must prove that they are unencumbered by criminal convictions or associates. Similarly, a hospital must prove that the CAT scanner it wants to install will not interfere with the business operations of another hospital, or a competing device in a so-called "catchment area"—an area defined both in square miles and by population—commonly a census tract, or perhaps a number of contiguous census tracts.

In the world of banking the standards are not much different. A license would not be forthcoming unless the applicant shows that it will not trigger competition that would be considered harmful to the entire banking system. The applicant normally would be required by both the state and federal authorities to submit voluminous data pertaining to the area in which the business is to be conducted: the population; its density; its median age; its savings patterns; employment statistics; area growth projections; and the size, location, and history of all competing facilities within a large radius of the proposed new banking facility. All of this information must be weighed, sifted, and evaluated so that a determination can be made as to whether or not the public convenience will be served.

As should be clear from these examples, public convenience is a concept designed and used by the governments to ensure healthy—not cutthroat—competition, and to promote the balance and mix of businesses, rather than the saturation of any one town with too much of what might otherwise be a good thing. If a little poetic license may be permitted, the states prune out some of the potential growth to insure that those who remain have ample space and sunlight to blossom to their fullest potential. In return, those who do remain must submit to both the rigors and the rewards of the hothouse environment that states create for them.

The critical factor on which all of these licensing decisions rest is density of population or the size of the market. The public policy is not to saturate towns with liquor stores. In the interest of this policy, a population-to-license ratio is set up as the controlling criterion. It is public policy to disallow hospitals to battle each other in providing high-tech services, with Medicare and Medicaid programs underwriting their fight. The wasteful confrontation is avoided by the states setting definitive licensing guidelines. Public policy is to ensure that banks are solvent, so the government never has to intervene. Banking regulators accomplish this goal by informally dividing the marketplace in the name of public convenience. Whatever the label, the underlying public policy is contingent on the common denominator of population per square mile or population density of the market. This is the key ingredient—the sine qua non—of the manner in which the government licenses and controls competition in all private and quasi-monopolies.

We are once again confronted with that gnawing public policy question: who is to regulate the putative regulators? Here the question is compounded, because the state is not only the alleged regulator, but is also the sole owner of an enterprise over which the exclusive legal rights are exercised. The state-run lottery is, as they say, the only game in town. The states' interests are not served by healthy, balanced competition, as is the case in other regulated industries. The state is so extremely jealous of its profitable monopoly that it has made competition not merely improper and, therefore, subject to restraint, but criminal and, thereby, subject to punishment.

What have the state-run lottery monopolies done in response to this patent public policy quandary? They have reverted to pretending that they are regulatory agencies. They dress themselves in the selfsame language that is used by the bank regulators, the liquor regulators, and the health facilities regulators.

New Jersey's statute is typical. Is says that the director is empowered to issue licenses to agents to sell tickets for the lottery as "will best serve the public convenience...," then follows the language which is considered to be the controlling mandate, "and promote the sale of tickets." This language is certainly not unique to New Jersey's statute.

Scientific Games, Inc., one of the largest beneficiaries of the existence of lotteries, has attempted to secure wider markets through expansion of the lottery to more states. It does this in various ways, ranging from lobbying individual legislators in nonlottery states, to organizing petition drives for public initiatives where they are allowed by state law. As part of their ongoing campaign they have drafted what they consider to be model legislation based on typical legislation already in place in many states. This more than likely will be the model used in any state which opts for a state-run lottery. The section of the model bill that reads as follows is pertinent to our discussion:

Sec 1042 *Selection of Lottery Game Retailers*

The Director shall, pursuant to this chapter and the rules and regulations of the Commission, select as Lottery Game Retailers such persons as deemed best to serve the public convenience and promote the sale of tickets or shares. No natural person under the age of 18 shall be a Lottery Game Retailer. In the selection of a Lottery Game Retailer, the Director shall consider factors such as financial responsibility, accessibility of the place of business or activity to the public, security of the premises, integrity, reputation, the sufficiency of existing Lottery Game Retailers for any particular Lottery Game to serve the public convenience, and the projected volume of sales for the Lottery Game involved.

Lawyers refer to phrases such as "the public convenience" as a "term of art." This means that as a result of long custom and usage, as well as court precedent, the term has obtained a universally accepted and specific meaning in the law. Every lawyer, every legislator, and certainly every judge knows what is meant by the phrase, the public convenience. By now, it is hoped that the reader has a fair grasp of the concept as well, so we might turn to some of the facts and data to determine just how well the public is being served by a system that has the director of each lottery playing the triple role of licensing authority, putative regulator, and profitmaking business executive at the same time.

According to a survey conducted in 1987 by *Gaming and Wagering Business* magazine, most states were aiming toward a goal of having one sales terminal, which would be tied into the state's main computer, for every 2,500 residents. However, ten states were hoping to build networks that would provide one terminal for every 1,200 to 1,500 residents. California, for instance, had 7,500 terminals in 1987, or one for every 3,491 residents, but wanted to double the number of terminals so that they would provide one terminal for for every 1,870 residents. Massachusetts already had one terminal for every 1,300 people, and intends to add another 100 terminals to lower the ratio to one to 1,250. New York had a ratio of one to 4,000, and had a target of one to 2,000. The Maryland ratio stood at one to 2,500 in 1987, but the state was hoping to reduce that to one to 2,000 as soon as possible.

It should be mentioned that companies which supply materials and supplies to the lottery operations, such as Scientific Games, Inc., recommend that the optimum ratio is one agent or outlet for every 1,000 of population. This type of advice is not unexpected from the people who are the greatest promoters of the lotteries.

Further, as well as more detailed, examination of the data will help reveal the real significance of these numbers.

The Delaware Council on Gambling Problems, headquartered in Wilmington, DE, conducted an intensive six-month study on "the impact of state-sponsored gambling on the community." The study was conducted between April 1 and September 30, 1979, and focused on a unit much smaller than the entire state. This particular study dealt only with one, albeit the largest, county, New Castle. At the time this study was conducted, there were only eighty-seven terminals located in the entire state of Delaware. This study has been attacked in some quarters for its methodology, which relied on personal interviews of approximately 1,500 people. While it might be granted that such a technique may allow for some distortion and skewing of data, the portion of the report to be dealt with here is invulnerable to such criticism, as it is based solely on objective demographics.

The Council concluded that "the State Lottery Commission has purposely placed its lottery machine locations in the poorest areas where there is the highest unemployment figures, the lowest standards of living and the highest percentage of welfare recipients:

a. There is not a single lottery machine in the highest income area of 17,630 persons. (Hockessin, Yorklyn, Centerville, Greenville)
b. There is one lottery machine for every 17,774 persons in the upper-middle income areas, or 6 machines for 106,648 persons. (Fairfax, Talleyville, Rockland, Arden, Winterthur)
c. There is one lottery machine for every 5,032 persons in the lower middle to middle working income areas, or 40 machines for 201, 316 persons. (Claymont, Stanton, Bellefonte, Elsmere, Newport, and parts of Wilmington)
d. There is one lottery machine for every 1,981 persons in the poorest income area, or 21 machines for 41,610 persons. (Wilmington: northeast/east/west center city/south city and the barrio)"

The figures and definitions used were from the United States Census Bureau, the Planning Offices of both the city of Wilmington and New Castle County, and Community Action for Greater Wilmington. Needless to say, this aspect of the study was never challenged. Delaware, at the time of this study, had been operating its lottery for five years. Over the next eight years, it added machines and, by 1987, claimed to provide one terminal for every 2,534 residents on a statewide basis.

A 1984 Maryland study showed that the city of Baltimore, with its population of 660,000 and a median household income of $16,800 enjoyed the convenience of 400 outlets, or about one for every 1,850 residents. Montgomery

County, with its 590,000 people enjoying median household incomes of almost $34,000, had only 101 outlets, or one for every 5,800 residents of that county. Maryland added 500 terminals between 1984 and 1987. One must wonder where they were placed, especially in light of the fact that Maryland's lottery director told *Gaming and Wagering Business* that growth rates should be determined by sales figures, past and projected, and not for the sake of improving the ratio of terminals to population.

The lottery operation in the District of Columbia tells a different, but more accurate, story about the prevailing policies of urban saturation than do the figures that only report statewide averages. In Washington, DC, according to the 1987 survey, the ratio was one to 1,000, with a projected target of one to 832.

Maybe this kind of disparity can be accounted for by the fact that lotteries, and particularly the daily numbers games, are perceived to be city games. In 1987, Edward Stanek, the director of the Iowa lottery, told *Governing* magazine that, "daily games are principally urban games, not for suburban or rural areas with little pedestrian traffic. Iowa had no market for a daily game. The numbers games also had been played illegally, for years, for generations, in the East. When they were legalized, they had a ready audience. There's no such history in the West."

Certainly, the urban centers of the nation's most urban state, New Jersey, were not found to be wanting for lottery outlets. The state's capital, Trenton, has 121 agents to serve its 92,000 residents, or one agent for each 750 of population. In the shadows of the casinos in Atlantic City there are 35 agents to serve the 37,000 full-time residents. Notwithstanding these examples, the report issued in the summer of 1988 defended the lottery outlet placement by citing: "12.6% of the Lottery agents are located in Essex County where 11% of New Jersey households are located. Eight percent of households are in Hudson county where 8.6% of Lottery agents are located." This data is simply misleading. Using percentage of households, as opposed to percentage of total population, makes the ratios look somewhat better than they are. But, the unspoken facts are what perhaps are the most relevant. Essex is a' county of nearly a million people, and contains what may be the wealthiest and the poorest neighborhoods in the entire state. The use of countywide figures conveys no essential information. To a significant degree, even citywide statistics can be misleading, since every large metropolitan center has areas of relative affluence as well as areas of poverty and blight.

Information that is misleading is merely objectionable, whereas outright falsehoods should be unforgivable. The Lottery Commission in New Jersey paid $275,000 for this report that concludes its discussion on location of outlets by stating, "the New Jersey counties (Essex, Hudson, Union, Passaic, and Bergen) with the highest number of black, Hispanic, and low-income households also contain the largest number of lottery agents. *This is because these counties have the largest number of households.*" This is not just misleading; it is grossly inaccurate. Three affluent suburban counties (Middlesex, Monmouth, and Morris) have larger populations than do Passaic and Union.

Normally, when challenged, lottery officials will point to statistics which indicate that the largest and most successful producers (that is, generators of sales), are located in suburbs and not in inner cities. They then argue that this proves that the bulk of the sales are taking place in the more affluent suburbs instead of in the acknowledged poorer areas of the cities. This may project a false picture of the pattern of lottery sales. It may be true that suburban outlets generate high sales, but that is because competition is at a minimum, with suburban retailers serving populations as much as 1,000 percent larger than their fellow lottery retailers in the inner cities. Another reason for suburban outlets to show extraordinary sales statistics is that they are near the border of a nonlottery state.

When does the standard of public convenience metamorphosize into saturation? And when does such saturation turn into simple exploitation? Certainly, if anyone were to suggest that the number of liquor stores should be increased to one for every 500 residents, there would be a public hue and cry that would shake the corridors of the statehouse. No banking regulators would permit uncontrolled branch proliferation to the point that every 500 people had the convenience of an office in their neighborhood, until the whole system collapsed around their heads. Licensing that would permit such a saturation would not be tolerated as public policy, but we have witnessed a licensing of lottery agents that clearly is a policy of saturation of poorer areas.

This is not a policy of public convenience, as that term has come to be known in the law through precedent, custom, and usage, but the policy of maximum sales to the market most prone to be vulnerable to regressive taxes. Where does this policy of proliferation end? This is more difficult to answer than the question of where it all began.

New Hampshire began distribution of its tickets on a very modest scale with only a handful of outlets, focusing its major sales efforts on its two licensed race tracks and its state-controlled liquor stores. When the state of New Jersey studied the operations of both New Hampshire and New York in 1970 prior to launching its own project, it concluded that both states had failed to have enough outlets and that tickets in New Jersey should be more widely available. The commissioners involved in that study were sure that tickets should be made available for sale at places where people tended to visit, such as the boardwalks in Atlantic City and Seaside Heights. They even briefly considered, but ultimately rejected, such ideas as selling tickets at the toll booths on the New Jersey Turnpike and Garden State Parkway, and at the motor vehicle offices. It is true that people visit these locations, but they already tend to congregate at them for inconveniently lengthy periods of time. The commission finally decided that the traffic tie-ups would not be in the best interests of the motoring public, and that motor vehicle offices had difficulties in handling what they were already doing. The commission also directed that a survey be undertaken to determine where potential buyers would like to see tickets made available. The survey was conducted by asking people to choose from a list of possible sales locations where they would prefer to see ticket outlets placed by the state. Possible choices were such places as shopping centers; drug stores; gas stations; newsstands; airport, rail, and bus terminals; liquor stores; bars and lounges; restaurants, hotels, and motels; state and municipal offices; race tracks; bowling alleys; and movie theaters. Each potential place had its partisans. Over the years, lottery directors have solved the placement dilemma simply by placing outlets everywhere imaginable.

Outlets have become a ubiquitous part of every urban landscape. One can be found at a one-hour cleaning shop on Route 1 in Elizabeth; and in one area of Trenton, there are three outlets within a space of 600 feet. In fact, in New Jersey, even an adult bookstore has obtained permission to dispense lottery tickets, albeit only after a hard-fought court battle. The fact that the lottery commission fought the matter in court is no reason to award them any accolades. The court ruled in favor of this nontraditional location only because the lottery commission had not developed or promulgated any regulations or criteria that would have justified denial of the application.

For the first decade of operation, most lotteries struggled to assure that all potential markets, particularly the urban areas, were covered. At their inception, the majority of the lotteries were able to emulate the early lessons of the lottery pioneers, such as New York and New Jersey. One of those lessons is to concentrate outlets in the cities, rather than in the suburbs. The other lesson is that despite representations about the benefits of the lottery as the potential salvation of the "mom-and-pop" neighborhood grocery store, lottery operators turn as quickly as possible to the major chain store operations. This has been the demonstrable case in the western states.

Washington state, for example, started its first game in November 1982. Six months later, state officials printed their first report boasting that they had paid sizable fees to retailers who had served as ticket agents during the crucial start-up period. Were these the small enterprises that needed the extra boost to insure their continued survival? Not exactly. Of the $7,750,000 paid out in ticket sales commissions, almost $1,000,000 went to Safeway stores. The next largest amount, $800,000, was paid to state liquor stores; however, they were delighted by the fact that the sales of their liquor inventory increased by 10 to 20 percent in this first six-month period because of lottery ticket sales. The specifics of this cause-and-effect phenomenon has not been analyzed, so it won't be suggested that maybe the losers were drowning their sorrows. These two sales leaders were followed by other large chain store operations—but no mom-and-pop stores.

Similarly, Colorado started its first lottery in January 1983. Its first report on the distribution of commissions found the Seven-Eleven convenience store chain in first place, with the following chain stores following: Safeway, King Super, Albertson's Loaf and Jug U/Tote/M, Vickers, Quick-Way, City Markets, Venta, and Royal Petroleum. The pattern was the same in Arizona, which commenced sales on July 1, 1981. In its first fiscal year, it reported that it paid sales commissions of slightly over $6,100,000 to its agents and retailers, with 70 percent of that amount being paid to twenty-five large chain store operations.

Supermarkets and convenience stores have become the major sales centers for lottery tickets throughout the country. Local newsstands and neighborhood grocery stores are still on the scene, as are liquor stores, but the trend is moving away from owner-operated stores. Chain operations, both of the convenience-store type as well as fast-food restaurants, are now major factors in the retail sales picture, and supermarkets are the dominant sales outlet nationwide. The states are happier with this new development, as it permits certain economies to be implemented. One of these economies is so clever that a special mention must be made of it.

It is not uncommon to see someone at the check-out counter with a cart so full of items that it will take a few minutes for the sales clerk just to ring them all up on the register. (Somehow, this person with these dozens of items is always just ahead of you in the line.) The person with all these purchases usually can be observed shifting from foot to foot or leafing through a newspaper or magazine as they wait for their goods to be rung up. Now, some supermarkets, and even smaller-sized convenience stores, are offering them an alternative way in which to spend those otherwise "dead" minutes. Player-activated lotto terminals have been installed right on the customer's side of the check-out counter. While the clerk is tabulating the purchases and bagging the groceries, the customer can buy lotto tickets and choose the numbers merely by pressing the appropriate keys on the player-activated terminal. All the clerk must do is press the total button on the cash register, and out comes your final statement, lottery-ticket purchases included. This method of selling tickets is truly "convenient," at least in the colloquial sense.

We have seen precisely what the term of art, the public convenience, means when applied to the licensing and control of private enterprises that enjoy monopolies and quasi-monopolies. Does it have a different meaning when the state applies the concept to itself? Review of the data and history allows for the following conclusions to be drawn:

1. The states have been interested in saturating markets, not in fostering competitive environments.
2. The states labeled terminal allocation decisions public policy; however, such decisions were no more than marketing strategy.
3. The states' public policies/marketing strategies are devoid of any sensitivity to social concerns, such as hiring priorities of the unemployed, economically disadvantaged, and physically limited.
4. The states are moving away from mom-and-pop stores and are expanding their sales networks in retail chain operations.
5. The states are deemphasizing labor-intensive sales efforts to concentrate on automated ticket distribution.

This brings us to the threshold of the future, where it is apparent that a marketing revolution is about to occur. In the next chapter, we will explore the potential for new marketing techniques that could be upon us before we realize it.

7

Marketing the Lotteries of the Future

In the world of gambling, the *ne plus ultra* of betting operations on this planet is the Royal Hong Kong Jockey Club which runs all legalized betting, on and off the track, in that Crown Colony. The operation is awesome. It is a fully computerized marvel of state-of-the-art efficiency, designed to make betting easy. It maintains 600,000 active accounts. This means that members of the club have charge accounts, also known as a bank, with the club. They can place their bets on both the races and daily numbers (i.e., lottery) by phoning the club's office. And now there is an important breakthrough of which to take note: the hand-held gambling computer which is presently being issued to the club's 150,000 most valued bettors. These are about the size of the average portable tape recorder, or Walkman cassette player. However, they do a great deal more than a tape player. The owner can use it to access all of the up-to-the-minute information on odds and such; and, more important to the club, it can then be used to place a wager, simply by punching in the numbers and then interfacing the computer to a phone line. The busy executive can, therefore, use his special device to bet the races and play the numbers while driving his car to the office in the morning. Once at work, they just hand the computer to someone in the office to plug it into the nearest phone jack. It can even be used in conjunction with the car phone. This innovation may well be just another electronic toy to amuse the affluent in the Orient or, on the other hand, it may well be the type of thing that, like many other such toys, will become common-place in the not too distant future.

The use of advanced technology will allow American lottery agents to do what those who run the Jockey Club in Hong Kong have already done to make their operation the best-run gambling operation in the world. Technology will allow lottery agents to cut overhead while retaining the best-qualified person-nel, and to handle the situation in which there is not an available labor pool to run the lottery operation. Automation and advanced technology may be an-swers to the prayers of more than a few lottery directors.

Before looking into the brave new world of future lottery operations, it would be useful to revisit the genesis of existing operations, paying careful attention to the sales psychology that prompted the present marketing patterns.

Early on, all lottery managers recognized the importance of at least two important marketing principles which apply to any new product or service: first, the need for grass-roots, community-based support; and second, the need to build product loyalty among consumers.

In the chapter on advertising, we see how the opinion-molders in many states were coopted by pro-lottery forces. A proviso was inserted into the initiative proposals that a certain percentage of gross ticket sales would be dedicated to ongoing promotion and advertising. This, of course, was designed to instill a high degree of enthusiasm into professional public relations experts who obviously could anticipate new work. It may also have chilled certain editorial opposition from media who could anticipate millions in new advertising dollars. It was, and remains, a clever strategy.

Much the same mentality is reflected in the manner in which distribution outlets were structured. The "mom-and-pop" retailers, as well as the large chains, foresaw the additional business they could generate from being the local lottery ticket retailer. The strategy worked exceptionally well, and lottery proponents found retailers, large and small, to be adamant and vocal allies in any campaign to adopt a lottery in a given state. The indigenous business person constituted the local grass-roots supporter that was of enormous value in states where the ballot initiative was the vehicle for authorizing a lottery. In those states where the lotteries were the result of direct action by the state's legislature, the retail business community played just as important a role, lobbying aggressively for adoption of the lotteries as a viable alternative to increased taxes, and promoting the lotteries as methods of helping marginal retailers in the older urban centers who often were facing stiff competition from new suburban malls. The arguments were cogent and vociferously advanced by those who saw their interests enhanced by becoming retailers of lottery tickets.

Indeed, the retail business sector was rewarded for its efforts, whether directed at the passage of a ballot initiative, or more narrowly focused on their state representative or senator. The time, effort, energy, and enterprise that they invested in promoting the lottery and obtaining their franchise to sell tickets was a good investment, at least until recently. More than $5 billion has been paid to retailers over the last two decades. While no precise figures are available for each of the twenty-nine states, it generally is accepted that a small retailer may earn between $100 and $250 a week in lottery commissions. A typical convenience store will make enough sales to receive about $500 in the same week. A supermarket, on the other hand, expects something closer to $1,000 per week in commissions. In New Jersey, for instance, the most successful outlet, a suburban pharmacy, sells an average of $28,000 worth of tickets each week, earning for itself $1,400. The lowest earners eke out less than $100 in the same time period.

No matter the present level of activity, after more than ten years of operation, the lottery is not dependent on the local agent for continued consumer loyalty to their product. If and when public interest in the lottery lags, operators do not look to their agents to stir up increased sales. States can resort immediately to the use of mass media and implementation of a new game. Agents are still in the picture, but their roles are no longer central to the promotion of the games. Consumers are clearly loyal to the product, not to the merchant.

Moreover, the state is not necessarily very loyal to its retailers. Too much success on the part of an agent often will be rewarded by the installation of another outlet in close proximity, the theory being that a rich vein has been struck in this particular community and should be mined for all it is worth. This mentality, of course, inexorably leads to saturation, again demonstrating that the state has no qualms about marketing in the most aggressive fashion—a fashion that also is clearly insensitive to the concerns of the individual agent, no matter how loyal or successful they have been.

Given the primacy of earnings over loyalty to agents, what might the future hold for the retail sellers of lottery tickets? Because consumer loyalty is to the product and not to the individual seller, and the agent is viewed by the state officials as just one more item of overhead, the days of the friendly neighborhood agent may be numbered. As the lotteries' marketing operations become ever more sophisticated, the retail outlets may well find themselves squeezed out of the process. The signs are already present in some areas.

The level of the commission is often set by statute, which provides some protection to the agent. But, in some states where the commission level is flexible, retailers in choice markets in some regions already are being told that they may face loss of their franchise if they are not willing to negotiate a lower commission arrangement with their state. So called "stand-alone terminals" and "player-activated terminals" clearly are devices that the state can use as another form of leverage to squeeze commissions from existing outlet owners. These machines function as their names imply—without the necessity of any agent. The player controls the entire process, inserting money and choosing the numbers to be played on a keyboard. The ticket is then dispensed automatically. The threat of widespread use of such machines gives the states bargaining power that intimidates even the most independent of agents.

Finally, states may establish state-owned-and-operated retail outlets, or give preferential treatment to chain operations, who agree to lower or discount commissions. One such chain operation already in existence has only one product—lottery tickets. The company proposes to set up kiosks in the parking lots of large malls and on downtown street corners and run operations similar to film-developing businesses—and do so for commissions that are lower than those paid to independent vendors.

Three additional trends can be identified:

1. Use of video games as adjuncts to the standard lottery games;
2. Use of telemarketing; and
3. Use of credit cards in association with purchase by telephones.

The retail community can, for the most part, be refined out of existence—such that its services are no longer needed, except in the rarest of instances. The television, the telephone, the computer, and the credit card have made small community enterprises potentially obsolete in terms of the lottery.

Why should the states continue to pay 5 or 6 percent of gross sales on an expense that can easily be eliminated with a modicum of capital costs? Remember, the commissions are a recurring annual expense. In terms of a billion-dollar sales operation, these commissions amount to $50,000,000. Boosting the bottom line by 5 percent in perpetuity is the kind of thing that builds a manager's reputation and earns for him enormous credit and rewards. If you want a glimpse of the future of lottery marketing, look no further than your television and telephone.

In New York, Off Track Betting (OTB) gives us a perfect idea of where lottery betting is going. It is another excellent way of getting a peek at the potential future. New York's operation is just a few years behind Hong Kong's, and probably a couple of years ahead of state lottery operations, but it points the way potentially to unlimited lottery growth, and unlimited abuse, as well. A bettor interested in "improving the species," as they say, is allowed to open an account with the legalized horse parlor. All one has to do is prove that he has money in a New York bank in a sufficient amount to cover the bets he is placing at the OTB office. In fact, after the account is opened the regular player no longer is faced with the inconvenience of having to stand in line at the OTB outlet. All one has to do is pick up the phone and call in one's bets. No bookie was ever more accommodating. The state of New York is so eager for the off-track-betting action that it attempts to make the entire transaction not only fast, private, and convenient, but also very businesslike; the state will even go so far as to keep all the records for the bettor. Just as ordinary people everywhere else expect that their bank will provide them with a monthly statement; so, too, the regular horse player in New York can have the benefit of a regular report indicating all wagers placed, together with a full breakdown of winners, losers, current balance, and more. The only thing that the state has not yet done is agree to go into the money-lending business; no credit is as yet available. But if the bettor agrees to maintain a balance of $1,000 or more, no surcharges are levied on winning bets. All bets must be backed either by money on deposit with the OTB office, or by money in a bank that the bettor has previously agreed may be levied on by the state in the event that the bettor doesn't make good quickly enough. How far off is something similar for lottery gamblers in New York and everywhere else?

From this unvarnished view of one form of legalized, state-operated gambling in our second largest state, it is possible to project how easily this technology could be adapted to the lottery operations. Let's start with the winners. If the win is over $600, it must be reported to the federal tax authorities, as well as to state officials if a state income tax is in effect. However, if the money were to be held by the state and kept on deposit for further betting, the withholding and reporting regulations might not apply. If unsuccessful bets dropped the net proceeds below the $600 figure, maybe the IRS need never know; in the meantime, the bettor can have the fun and excitement of additional plays. Moreover, one of the most trusted tenets of the lottery is that winners keep playing, and that a large portion of most Pick 3 and Pick 4 winnings will find their way back into the betting pool on future days. Therefore, it makes eminently good sense for the lottery programs to initiate a method whereby lottery winners may keep their winnings on deposit with the state and use it as a credit for future ticket purchases. If the results of the 1988 New Jersey telephone survey are to be believed, a full 69 percent of all "winnings from lottery games were used to buy more tickets..."

The potential scenario for how this might start is easy to imagine. A code number will be issued with great fanfare to some big winner; complete with a huge press conference and lots of smiling faces in the photos, and the winner can then just pick up the phone, dial a special number, and place a bet.

Shortly after the first code number is issued and the first credit account is programmed into the mainframe, the program will be offered to every winner of even relatively small amounts. Finally, participation will be open to everyone. It probably will start with a $100 deposit for those not so lucky to have won recently. The states ultimately will push the program very aggressively. Bookkeeping expenses will be nominal compared to the 5 or 6 percent sales commission presently being paid out to the agents. Even more important is the extra money the state would be able to make on the "float." For those not conversant with the term, it applies to the fact that on large amounts of money, interest is paid on a daily basis sometimes for use overnight. The state would keep on deposit your winnings or the money you've sent them to open an account for you. They, in turn, would use your money to make extra money for themselves. It could be defined as backdoor banking, but the lottery operations have already been doing it for years, and they are not the only division of state government that engages in the practice of investing money that really belongs to the citizenry in order to get a little extra interest for themselves. All of this is contingent on the concept of the "time-value of money."

If this isn't perfectly clear yet, consider this example. Tokens for use at toll booths, whether they be on roads or mass transit, are sold to the public on the basis that they are designed to expedite travel. This simply is not true. They are sold solely so that the authority can get your money in advance, in order to invest it and earn interest while waiting for you to toss the token into the toll booth or turnstile. You buy $10 worth of tokens. It is insignificant to you as a single individual; however, assume that there are 1,000,000 others in similar positions. On the first of the month, the authority gets $10 million which it immediately puts in the bank to earn interest. In the meantime, you and a million others are walking or driving around with tokens in your possession which are not the equivalent of real money. This is a subtle variant on the term "economy of scale." Remember, at any given time, there are 100 million or more New York subway tokens floating around somewhere unaccounted for, while the Transit Authority has the cash in the bank earning interest. If it works so well for mass transit systems, it can work just as well, or better, for the lottery operations.

Once again, just as we can point to the first hints of commission squeezing in the deals that are being struck by some states with chain store operators, we can point to the subscribe-by-mail efforts as examples of both direct marketing and the state taking advantage of the float. Subscription by mail is offered in many states, and involves the bettor exercising various options. One of the most popular is one which provides for the bettor to send in an annual subscription on one specific number. The player, then, has that number in every single daily number drawing for the number of drawings he has paid for—in advance. The state likes this because not only have they saved the commission, but they also have the money to invest and to earn interest while the subscriber waits for the number to hit.

The day when the majority of lottery sales take place by phone is not far off. As far as the lottery directors are concerned, it can't come soon enough, for it truly would be one of the most clever double plays ever seen in an industry famous for clever maneuvers. The lottery operations would be saving money by cutting down commissions on one side of the ledger. The second part of the double play is that the state would be keeping millions of dollars on deposit for thousands of individual players paying out no interest while having the money earning interest for the lottery itself.

What about the poor areas where few, if any, have private phones, no less credit cards? Despite protestations that the so-called "new generation" of lottery game, the video lottery, was designed for the yuppie market, it is clearly geared for the poor. The video lotteries are just what the name implies; they are a cross between a slot machine, a pinball machine, and a computer. Put money in and win or lose on the spot. This is alleged to be extremely attractive to the young single set with extra money to spend at their local cocktail lounge. Of course, such devices could be placed virtually everywhere. These video games are also merely supplementary to currency-operated vending machines that dispense lottery tickets automatically for games such as the weekly lotto drawings. Some machines are sophisticated enough to sell daily-drawn tickets. Why these devices in the presence of 80,000 living, breathing agents? The answers are as simple as they are cynical.

Automatic vending machines and video lotteries have enormous advantages over agents, the first being sales twenty-four hours a day. This, of course, is the ultimate dream of any marketing operation. When the shopping centers have closed, the convenience stores have closed the doors, the newsstands have sold their final papers or packs of cigarettes, even after the lounges and taverns have turned out their lights and said good night to the last patrons, the lottery could still be selling tickets and offering games in the all-night diners, truckstops, or bus, train, and airline terminals. The machines could be placed on the streets just as papers are sold in many places already.

The second great advantage to such automation is the reduction or elimination of agents' commissions.

The third advantage is one of particular appeal in the high-volume, but crime-ridden, inner cities. No personnel are placed at risk during dangerous hours. Those critical hours between sundown and sunrise are ripe for gambling, but no one has to keep their business open to sell tickets.

These, of course, are the principle reasons that automation makes sense for lottery operators in the inner city. In the suburbs, the same reasons apply, with the exception that crime fears are not as prevalent.

What is prevalent in the suburbs is the electronic cottage, where we can bank by phone, shop by phone, transfer funds on our home computers, and plug in our modems to connections all over the world. There, we can pick up our phone, dial for information on sports and weather, or just talk to people hooked into the same conversation line. We can watch a debate on TV and immediately record our reactions by calling the respective numbers, pro or con, as shown on the screen. How far distant is the day when we can bet over the phone, buy our lottery tickets on one credit card or another, or just tell them simply to put it on our phone bill in the form of a toll call? Or, best of all in the view of the lottery operators, just say, "Charge it to my state lottery account."

Agents should recognize that they are rapidly being rendered obsolete by the exploding technological advances being made daily. As pressures build for increased revenues, it is the commission segment of the expense side of the lottery balance sheet that is the most vulnerable. It is axiomatic in commerce that one of the simplest ways to save money is to cut out the middle persons— the brokers, the agents—and deal directly with the customer. As we have seen, the loyalty is to the product and not to the merchant.

A few last words are in order to finalize the point: The product here is not tangible. It doesn't come in a can, a bottle, or a package. No one has to stop off and pick up a ticket, as one must shop for food or clothing. There would be absolutely no necessity for anyone to go to a store to buy a ticket when they have the option of merely picking up the phone or punching in a few numbers to be transmitted by their computer modems. It will be more convenient and more efficient. In fact, "tele-betting" will be the ultimate in public convenience, but we must decide now, before it happens, whether it reflects wise public policy.

8

Advertising the Lotteries: Present Practices

We have seen from previous chapters that the lottery is actually an unregulated state monopoly, functioning in a social policy vacuum, with its only dynamic being the ever-increasing need to sell more tickets. The answer, therefore, to an inquiry into who sets advertising policy is that no one sets policy, but rather policy is set for the states by their self-imposed imperative to raise more revenue through increased sales. Restraining the legitimate flow of information to consumers is an intractable problem, made even thornier by the fact that the states are caught in the bind of being protectors of consumers on the one hand and marketers of a specific product on the other. This chapter examines some of the current advertising practices and identifies some of the more obvious problems that confront policymakers.

Adam Smith described in detail the balancing of supply and demand and the fine economic minuet they perpetually dance. State-operated lotteries have accelerated the tempo and distorted Smith's model in two obvious ways: (1) The state has a monopoly on the supply of lottery tickets and, therefore, faces no legal competition; and (2) The supply of tickets being theoretically unlimited, the state must continually stimulate demand.

What happens when the demand lags? We have seen in previous chapters how both budget projections and the raw need of the revenue place the states in a position where this cannot be allowed to occur. If, indeed, the demand should lag, the state cannot permit the normal market forces to operate, since such forces might result in a downward drift in the level of betting activity. This would be intolerable for state budgets, since the money has already been appropriated. In effect, the funds either have been spent or promised well in advance. Therefore, the states are always prepared to intervene to stimulate the demand.

In California, even the zeal of the state's officials was not left to chance. After all, the state had not yet had the opportunity to become addicted to the narcotic effect of the lottery revenue stream. In case Governor George

Deukmejian and his attorney general John Van de Kamp continued to be squeamish about "pushing people to gamble" or "using suckering kinds of techniques," as they previously had expressed their respective concerns, the initiative proponents wrote into the proposition the requirement that at least 3.5 percent of the gross revenue be allocated for "advertising, promotion, public relations, incentives, and other aspects of communication." It can be seen from this phraseology that lottery advocates believed that "money talks."

Gross receipts were anticipated to be $1 billion, so the 58 percent of the electorate in California, who supported the intiative in the face of the governor's opposition, knew in advance that at least $35 million would be spent annually to ensure that their own interest did not lag. This particular provision of the 1984 initiative proposal encouraged the prospective beneficiaries of this huge budget to enthusiastically campaign for voters' approval. It literally turned loose the creative juices of every public relations firm in the entire state of California.

Whatever the dynamics of the actual voting, it is central to the present discussion to focus on the full acknowledgment that large amounts of money are spent to ensure the selling of lottery tickets. The promoters of the California lottery were certainly in earnest about ensuring its success; because of the availability of the initiative option, the drafters of the proposition were, in effect, able to establish the exact public policy to be adhered to by the state's officials. Similar language has appeared in other initiatives, and it is inserted for the reasons outlined above. But most states don't have officials with the same high level of reluctance as Governor Deukmejian's, and, certainly, once the dollars start to flow there are, indeed, few nay-sayers. The revenue becomes irresistible, addictive. Even the misgivings of former opponents rapidly disappear, to be replaced with glowing predictions about the money that will be raised from the lottery in the coming year.

What this means is that the state, as a matter of public policy, must see to it that a certain amount of tickets are sold even if the buying public has indicated by its purchasing habits that it is disinclined to buy more tickets. The pattern has been for the states to stimulate sales in two ways: first, by the introduction of new games; and second, by increasing advertising. These two marketing tools are most often seen in combination, but if no new game is to be put into operation, then we witness not only an increase in advertising but a change in the level of its intensity, repetition, and saturation.

We saw in chapter 3 the success achieved by the initial introduction of the lotto game. Concentrating on the single issue of advertising, we can begin with the proposition that, in a free society, choices in the marketplace have some relevance to the self interest of the consumer. People rarely buy what they don't think they need, and it is rarer still to see the willing purchase of something the person does not really want. Buyers, as they make choices, are normally governed by what could be called the benefit factor. In other words, the buyer perceives that whatever service or product they are buying will have some benefit to them. Most important of all is the conviction held by the buyer that the perceived benefit is, at the very least, marginally predictable. Repeat sales and product loyalty are reinforced in classic Pavlovian, stimulus–response, fashion. If, indeed, the purchased item produces the gratification that the buyer looked forward to, then repeat sales normally will occur. Advertisers aspire to create buying patterns that are reflexive, requiring no conscious thought, but merely needing the prospective buyer to be properly and adequately stimulated. There also exist buyers of lottery tickets who require absolutely nothing but an open sales outlet. (Ann Landers wrote recently in her syndicated column responding to a woman whose husband, Jim, consistently spent half his paycheck on lottery tickets, notwithstanding the fact that, over the past five years, he had only won $87. Ms. Landers advised contacting Gamblers Anonymous. It should also be mentioned that in the context of effective tax rates, Jim was paying a lottery tax excise rate of 99.99 percent.)

How does one build product loyalty and repeat sales of a product that doesn't provide the anticipated benefit factor very often? This is a challenge to even the most creative and ingenious.

We can get a clear picture of how this challenge is met by reviewing the candid testimony of an advertising executive before the Senate Hearing in 1984. Mr. Edward Trahan, the public relations and advertising consultant for the Maryland State Lottery, in testifying before the U.S. Senate's Subcommittee on Intergovernmental Relations at the Hearing held on October 3, 1984, told Senator Durenberger of Minnesota the following:

> A lottery ticket has characteristics which find no parallel in the world of product or service advertising. Any product or service which comes to mind exists because it delivers a predictable benefit to the consumer, however marginal that benefit may be. Product loyalty is built into the consumer's behavior because time after time he experiences some kind of gratification or reinforcement.

> Advertising plays a critical role in reminding, promising, and reinforcing the reasons a consumer should utilize a particular service or product. Conventional advertising strategies which would be most effective with a typical consumer product do not apply to the lottery industry, because lottery tickets do not have the characteristics of the average consumer product.

> The inescapable fact of the probability tells us that the great majority of ticket consumers will experience failure after failure. In this context, the idea of continuity in an advertising campaign over a long period of time will not encourage an increase in sales.

Mr. Trahan undoubtedly is correct in asserting that conventional advertising is not appropriate for a product as unique as a lottery ticket. He is also probably accurate in observing that continuity in an advertising theme will not result in an increase in sales, but he offers no opinion on what role, if any, advertising plays in the buying habits of dedicated players. However, he does recognize that there are certain marketing techniques that actually can have a negative impact on sales. Here is what he had to say about that:

> Unlike advertising a consumer product where constant exposure of the brand reinforces the experience of satisfaction and invites the consumer to relive that satisfactory experience, constant exposure of a lottery ticket and agent location has the opposite effect. It reminds the majority of the purchasers that they didn't win, creating a negative impression that inhibits repeat purchases.
>
> Since it is ineffective and most often counterproductive to advertise a lottery ticket as a product, we have created a series of television and radio commercials which highlight the fun of playing the game and take the onus away from gambling. *We want to feed the consumers' need for fun and excitement propelling the fantasy which motivates them to buy the next ticket.* (emphasis added)

Some extremely relevant questions might be, Who told this talented gentleman what market to aim at, and what messages to convey? Who was it in the state of Maryland that had set the standards? And if, in fact, there were standards, what were they?

The facts and figures of lottery advertising demonstrate the significance of the power wielded by those having the control over the authorization of expenditures.

Gaming and Wagering Business's third annual advertising report states that lottery ad budgets remained relatively flat in fiscal year 1987. However, in the very first paragraph of the article we are advised that, "advertising expenditures for the twenty-three U.S. lotteries should top $156.4 million in fiscal 1987, a 26.4 percent leap over fiscal 1986." This is, indeed, a strange way to define "flat." In fairness, the story goes on to report that the five Canadian lotteries were increasing their advertising budgets by only 3.3 percent, and that established U.S. lotteries were holding down advertising budgets as sales flattened out. It is ironic that gross sales for the twenty-three states increased only 2.8 percent, while advertising, as they said, took a 26.4 percent "leap." At the same time, the figures were almost exactly reversed for the five lotteries in Canada, where sales jumped 27.4 percent and advertising increased by only 3.3 percent.

Television, according to the article, was the dominant medium in both the United States and Canada, soaking up 42.6 percent and 37 percent of the respective budgets. Radio was second, the print medium third in the states, while print medium was second and radio third in Canada. These top three forms of advertising consumed nearly 70 percent of the totals in all states and provinces. In the United States, the two rather ill-defined categories of "public relations" and "other," accounted for over 8 percent or almost $13 million. In Canada, this category of expenses accounted for only 3 percent of the total expenditures. Perhaps the categories of public relations and other were the areas wherein the lottery operations covered the monies that were actually spent on market research.

California, which spent over $40 million in 1986, cut back to $35.3 million in 1987. That amounted to $1.35 per person in that state, an amount lower by far than the $5.77 per person spent in Washington DC. The average cost per capita in the twenty-three states was $1.15. Maryland, where the lottery director had expressed such pride in low advertising costs to the same subcommittee of the U.S. Senate that Mr. Trahan was testifying before back in 1984, was unable to hold the line. In 1987, Maryland increased its expenditures by more than 42 percent and spent almost 5.5 percent of gross sales on advertising.

While the majority of states claim that their lottery advertising is restrained and tasteful, only a handful of states have established policies that specifically restrain aggressive advertising.

The magazine *Gaming and Wagering Business* also has been running an annual contest for the best lottery advertising campaigns. The magazine's editors are very candid people, but they do not report on which states finished at the bottom of the list. Over the years there has been some advertising that was so tacky that even lottery directors in other states could not restrain themselves from criticism. The poor taste exhibited by some states' advertising is almost legendary. New York and Illinois, for instance, were the targets of criticism from other lottery directors, and, as we shall see, such criticism was not unwarranted.

New York, for the last year or so, ran an intense radio campaign featuring the theme "fairy tales can come true." In the spring of 1988, New York introduced a new game called Keno, and started hyping it by telling radio listeners that, among other things, the "e" in Keno stands for the excitement you get from just playing the game, even if you don't win.

New Jersey's lottery director, Barbara Marrow, contends that her state uses fewer "hard sell" tactics. In a November 1987 interview, she told the *Star-Ledger*, "We use common sense and good taste." She went on to contrast her strategy with a billboard erected by the Illinois lottery several years ago in a Chicago ghetto. The sign said: "This could be your ticket out." Director Marrow told the paper, "If I put that up in Newark, I'd be tarred and feathered. You don't do that kind of stuff. It's tasteless."

What Director Marrow found to be acceptable by her standards was an ad that showed a popcorn and soda vendor working at a ball game trying to deal with three customers at once. With a terribly harried look on his face, his hat askew, and his tray about to fall, the message reads, "If I win Pick 6, I won't have to do this anymore." These print ads were just part of a general advertising campaign, whose principle message was this: Jobs requiring physical labor won't be necessary if you win the lottery. A series of half-completed billboards went up with a message scrawled reading: "I don't have to do this job! I just won the lottery."

No doctors, lawyers, or stock brokers have ever been shown in this campaign walking away from their jobs as a result of having just won the lottery. Only unskilled and semiskilled jobs were projected as being of the type that people wanted to or would abandon in the event of winning.

This example vividly illustrates a major theme in lottery advertising—denigration of the work ethic. It is this theme that is perhaps more pernicious than the fantasy theme to which it is a natural corollary.

Work and everything associated with it are major targets of lottery advertising campaigns. Subtly, the point is made that work is only for the unlucky. Work is always shown as something that lacks dignity and purpose. Work, in these ads, is depicted as menial, unfulfilling and unrewarding. Is this somehow a vision of the new American ethic?

Many of us are of an age that we can still recall when the work ethic was a hallmark of our society. An unquestioned and unchallenged value, glorified by our leaders, sanctioned by religious teachings, embodied in the tales of Horatio Alger, and the moral of many a tale from McGuffey's Readers, work was what had made us as a nation great, rich, noble, and strong. We worked harder and outproduced the rest of the world. Apparently, it is now totally out of fashion. But is it? Certainly not, to hear our leaders speak. Throughout the 1980s, both political parties have made the creation of new jobs, economic expansion, retraining, increased productivity, and increased competitiveness, the staples of their platforms. Ironically, the promotion of these attributes of the national character is left to poorly attended meetings of civic organizations or for after-dinner speeches in front of well-dressed, well-heeled audiences. At the same time that increased productivity and competitiveness either is being encouraged in front of limited audiences or is being preached to the already faithful, the anti-work ethic message is being broadcast to millions each day.

One of the elements of advertising upon which there is little, if any, dispute is that repetition of the message has an important and enduring effect. Jingles are recognized as being particularly effective in this regard. Lottery directors are relatively candid in admitting that their advertising efforts are designed to build product loyalty while, at the same time, they attempt to broaden their potential market by constantly introducing new players to the thrill and excitement of gambling. At the same time, are they, in fact, inculcating younger generations with an attitude that work is inappropriate and unpleasant? It is certainly a question that deserves much greater attention than it has previously received. The newspaper columnist, Andy Rooney, now best known for his normally testy commentary on CBS's "60 Minutes," posed the following question: "How can we teach kids that hard work is the way to success if they hear radio commercials paid for by their government suggesting that the way to get rich is to bet on a number? How can Americans who profess to believe in such classic virtues as honesty, thrift, hard work and intelligent action allow any part of the government they formed to run a gambling operation?"

Perhaps the real issue here is the one that has been raised time and time again in any investigation of how the state lotteries actually function: Who is making the decisions? Who is setting policy? And if a policy actually exists, what is it? Finally, has the potential impact of the lotteries' persistent and unrelenting attack on the work ethic ever been considered?

A review of the available literature does not reveal any studies of this phenomena, which, for lack of a better term, must be referred to as work-ethic bashing. It is strongly suggested that an intense review of this problem would be in order. H. Roy Kaplan, professor from Florida State University, has written a number of articles on lotteries, and has published an entire book based on interviews with lottery winners. In the summer of 1985 he published an article entitled "Lottery Winners and Work Commitment: A Behavioral Test of the American Work Ethic." The article appeared in *The Journal of the Institute for Socioeconomic Studies*. While useful to the extent that it tells us something about the behavior of the winners, Kaplan's study is extremely limited in its ability to tell us about the work attitudes of the millions of players who are still hoping to win. The test, referred to in the subtitle, examined whether lottery winners continued working after winning sizeable amounts of money. He arrived at two major findings:

1. Only 26 percent of the winners and their spouses left the work force through retirement or resignation in the year after they won.
2. The number of people who changed their work behavior increased as the size of their winnings increased.

While there is nothing startling in these findings, there are a number of problems that must be raised with the test itself. To begin with, only 576 responded to the 2,319 questionnaires that were mailed. Was this really a broad enough sampling on which to base any conclusions? Second, more than 10 percent of the questionnaires were returned by the post office as undeliverable. Doesn't this, in itself, tell us something about how people behave after they win? Moreover, 25 percent of the winners weren't working when they won. One does not need the benefit of academic studies to realize that having money changes the way people look at things. I am reminded of the famous exchange between James Dean and Elizabeth Taylor in the movie *Giant*. The wealthy woman portrayed by Ms. Taylor admonishes the penurious wildcatter played by Mr. Dean that "money isn't everything." He smilingly replies, "No ma'am, not when you got it."

It is somewhat contradictory for our elected leaders to agonize over trade deficits and the need to make our nation productive and competitive while, at the same time, hundreds of millions of dollars are being spent, often by these same officials, to encourage lottery sales by bashing the same work ethic that they so ardently extol.

Thus far, we have dealt with two familiar problems that are easily recognized by anyone who has seen or heard even a handful of lottery commercials. First, most lottery advertising is fantasy, attempting to lure the prospective player into a world of unreality and to ignore the enormous odds against them. The second, and perhaps more serious, problem is that the tone of most lottery advertising is often antiwork.

The timing of the lottery advertising also is a matter of concern. Admittedly, the timing of lottery commercials is a subtle proposition, but it is part of the entire piece, and equally as questionable as other aspects of lottery advertising campaigns.

Is there anything that you have ever noticed about the time of each month that lottery advertising seems to be most intense? Pay close attention and keep your eyes and ears open the next time you tear off a sheet from the calendar. Social Security checks are timed to arrive on the first of each month, and the same is true for many other checks that are a part of both our entitlement programs, such as pensions, veteran's benefits, unemployment, and workers' compensation, as well as public assistance. The practice is callous, and we all would like to think better of our government; but the reality of it is that advertising increases noticeably in direct ratio to the amount of public money that predictably is in circulation.

This relationship was first recognized as far back as 1979 in the study conducted in New Castle County, Delaware. The Council on Gambling Problems monitored various radio stations and newspapers and found that the number of lottery ads and commercials doubled on the first and second day of each month. The pattern hasn't changed over the past eight years. If anything, it has become more apparent that lottery commercials of all types are front-loaded at the beginning of each month to coincide with the receipt of government checks.

The fourth aspect of advertising policy that warrants attention is the market to which the advertising is targeted. Just as society itself can be structured and classified, so too can advertising markets be arranged to define where on the economic scale the message is aimed. Proving once again the truth of Foucault's maxim that "taxonomy is destiny," there is upscale advertising for the wealthy and downscale advertising for the bottom of the economic ladder.

If you happen to prefer classical music and keep your radio tuned into a station that has such a format, it is highly unlikely that you have ever heard a lottery commercial. If your preference runs to rhythm-and-blues or country-western music, then it is predictable that you have been deluged with lottery messages. If you take a train to work from an affluent suburb, you will see no lottery posters in the waiting room, but if you stand at a bus stop shelter in the inner city, you have a good chance of seeing a poster or sign concerning the lottery. The bus itself, if its route is through the city, might even have a lottery ad on its side or rear. Don't bother to look for similar advertising in the suburbs; it simply is never to be found there.

Have you ever thumbed through the *Wall Street Journal* or *Barron's* to check out the lottery ad? Don't bother; but if you really are interested in finding ads on a predictable basis, it is strongly recommended that you find out what paper has the largest ethnic readership. If the paper is published in Spanish, you are guaranteed to find an ad in almost every single edition. It should be added that this applies equally to other media such as billboards and posters at bus stops located in neighborhoods with heavy concentrations of Hispanics. The ads, by the way, are in Spanish, and their translation into English isn't always easy. Take, for example, the ad that appeared in urban areas of New Jersey in 1988 which read "Bono en efectivo." This doesn't mean "good and effective," but rather, "bonus in effect." In the New York subways, there presently are posters which picture a man and woman with eight children standing alongside a large brass bed in what clearly appears to be a tenement room. The slogan says in Spanish, "The New York Lottery helped me realize the American Dream." Who wrote this and who approved it? Why is this market so intensely targeted? The answer is simple. The studies that have been undertaken are so intensive and extensive that the states know literally everything there is to know about each market. You may recall that the data, using the widely accepted participation index, indicated that Hispanic-Americans bought tickets at a rate in excess of the rate that would reflect their percentage of the total population. This particular community actually should be an easy sell, given the fact that lotteries are such an integral part of the cultures of the numerous Spanish-speaking countries. The heavy advertising that we see in Hispanic communities may be the result of the necessity to overcome the resistance to American lotteries, with their high odds and few prizes.

How do the states know so much? Few subjects have been researched with the same professional expertise, nor with more determined zeal than the subject of who is the steady lottery player. However, instead of using the information to attempt to encourage more sales in the upscale markets that the states know they are failing to reach, the states are satisfied to continue to concentrate their advertising dollars on the very same lower-scale markets that are already buying more than their share of the tickets. This advertising is lazy at best, callous and cynical at worst, and unquestionably inefficient.

Advertising is focused on fantasy, attacks the work ethic, is timed to encourage heavy participation by those on social security, and is targeted to the poor. It is now appropriate to pose the question one more time: Who is supervising all this? Ask the lottery directors and they will explain that the industry is self-regulated and has been since the mid-1970s. At that time, the few states that were operating lotteries joined together to form what was then known as the National Association of State Lotteries, which, in turn, promulgated an Advertising Code of Ethics. Bearing in mind that this code has existed since 1975, it is still interesting to read it if only for its quaint naivete. Here is the entire Code:

Preamble
The National Association of State Lotteries hereby establishes an Advertising Code of Ethics for the purpose of self regulating the sale and promotion of State Lotteries and their various products. The Code establishes guidelines to insure truth in advertising; to provide for the full and complete disclosure of prize structures and odds; to insure compliance with law and media industry codes and standards and to provide ethical and beneficial information to the public.

Membership in the NASL shall be contingent in part on each member's strict adherence to this Code of Ethics and any violations thereof shall be referred to the Committee on Ethics of the NASL. Any questions regarding planned programs, products or the content thereof may be referred to the Committee on Ethics for evaluation and guidance.

A. General
1. Truth in Advertising
No member shall knowingly approve or authorize or employ any advertising on behalf of its lottery or any of its products which is false, misleading or otherwise deceptive as a means of encouraging the purchase of any lottery ticket or service. This rule shall apply to both words of copy and graphic illustration.

2. Standards of Good Taste and Behavior
All material prepared for the advertising and promotion of the State Lottery products and services shall reflect accepted standards of good taste and behavior. Such material may at no time or for any reason place emphasis on sex or sexual implications, ethnic consideration, physical disability or illness or any other untoward element which is distasteful or offensive to the public conscience.

3. Avoidance of Greed and Avarice
Greed or avarice may not be suggested as a reason to participate in Lottery games or services.

4. Exhortations to Bet
No member shall unduly exhort the public to bet by the engaging in advertising or other promotional activities which misrepresent by any means, directly or indirectly, a lottery participant's chances of winning any prize, or which denigrate people who do not buy lottery tickets or unduly praises people who do buy tickets. It shall be a violation of this rule to use unqualified or inaccurate language regarding a potential winner's winnings (e.g. "Buy a ticket and be a winner").

5. Full Disclosure

Complete and full disclosure of the total prize structure and the odds of winning in each category shall be prominently published and circulated at the outset of all Lottery games. The information should appear clearly and conspicuously in tabular form in either the initial "launch" advertising created to introduce a game or in the point of purchase brochure or both. The tabular statement of the prize structure shall include for each prize:

(a) The prize amount

(b) the number of prizes per million tickets (or per 100,000 or other appropriate number)

(c) The odds of winning each prize

(d) Any special restrictions pertaining to the prize (e.g., "Lifetime prize payments start at age 18 years or older and are paid for a minimum of 20 years.")

Such information must be readily available to the public at all times during any game. All restrictions imposed on Lottery participation and prize eligibility shall be prominently displayed in advertising where practicable. Player eligibility or age, claiming deadline, method of payment and other restrictive element must be clearly stated.

B. Compliance with Law

No member shall engage in advertising or promotional practices which violate applicable local, state or federal law.

C. Media Codes

All advertisements prepared for broadcast on radio or television shall adhere to the National Association of Broadcasters Television Code and Radio Code rules concerning state conducted lotteries adopted in January, 1975.

This code is honored only in its continuous breach. It would be more accurate to say that it is simply ignored.

The very existence of this code seems to fit into the same pattern that is constantly found with regard to the lotteries. There is a veneer, a gloss, that exists, the purpose of which is to give the surface impression that all is in order, and that there is nothing to be concerned about. Beneath the surface glimmer of Ethics and Advertising Codes and regulatory statutes, lies an unregulated, unbridled, unexamined, and unmitigated exercise in pure unadulterated avarice. Now avarice as a characteristic of private enterprise may only be distasteful; but when it becomes the centerpiece of the states' revenue policy, perhaps it is time that some rethinking both of our public policy and of our social policy be undertaken.

Part of the gloss, of course, is that promotions always be in good taste. The problem with honoring this aspiration was best expressed in a moment of candor by Howard E. Varner, Governor Deukmejian's appointee to launch the California Lottery. In a 1985 interview with the Los Angeles *Times* he said, "I think it [advertising] should always be done in good taste; [but] I don't know what good taste is."

In fact, what more Americans have seen than any other lottery commercial is what is known as the "ZAP" ad. It was created by W. B. Doner & Co., the agency hired by the Michigan State Lottery. It is designed to counteract the disclosure that your chances of being struck by lightning are ten times higher than your chance of winning a pick-six lotto game. The man on the TV screen is adamant about not buying a lottery ticket as he says, "I've got a better chance of being struck by lightning." A thunderbolt strikes him with a loud and colorful zap. Scorched, but alive, he has been converted, and says, "One ticket please." So much for good taste.

The states do, indeed, rely on the persuasiveness of odds as they try to dissuade people from driving while drinking, or, on the other hand, attempt to persuade teenagers to stay in school. In these types of public-service commercials probabilities are an essential part of the messages. Those messages are: If you drink and drive the odds are against you; and if you drop out of school the odds are against you. The state should not be sending such mixed signals. Either the statistical probabilities mean something, or they don't. If one can laugh off the odds on winning the lotto, one can just as easily laugh off the odds against being killed while driving drunk. Imagine a commercial in which a staggering drunk is playing with his car keys while saying, "I know my chances of getting home safely are the same as being struck by lightning."—zap— "Well, maybe I'll give it a try anyway."

Another aspect of the gloss of lottery advertising is the ubiquitous public service ads that are associated with lottery operations. This type of advertising is allegedly justified by the necessity for telling the electorate where the lottery dollars are being spent. Once again, credit should be given to the very clever public relations agencies that advise the numerous lottery commissions, and their directors. They were, in effect, handed a lemon and have made lemonade. As the states which already had lottery operations in place were confronted with the necessity to raise additional money during the recession of the early 1980s through increased taxes, the public demanded to know "what happened to the lottery money?" The question was so persistent that it became apparent that this question would have to be answered by more than the traditional brochures. To some extent, the problem for the states was largely of their own making. They continually had been cranking out stories about how great their operation was and how many people were winning big jackpots. The public had every reason to believe that the lotteries were generating lots of money.

The lotteries usually are the one and only aspect of a state's revenue raising activities that is the subject matter of daily news releases. The tax collectors rarely, if ever, acknowledge that they are doing well. It is a true rarity to see a story that says that sales tax or income tax revenues are increasing, or a story that has a state treasurer bragging about how cigarette or liquor receipts are better than expected. The relative health of the state's treasury is usually a matter of divination to be inferred from the published data on such things as employment levels and car sales.

With the lottery it is totally different, since games are state-run. No intricate reasoning is required to figure out that, as stories appear daily reporting a growing jackpot or the latest instant millionaire, people immediately make the connection—the state is getting richer. It was not, therefore, totally unexpected that the question would become more persistent: "What happened to the lottery money?"

Initially, this was regarded as a nuisance, and some state officials were so bold as to admit that maybe the lottery had been oversold. Apparently, there were millions of people out there who had the distinct misconception that the lottery generated revenues on par with sales taxes or income taxes.

Something had to be done. At first, the states attempted public information campaigns with simple straightforward efforts to put the facts on the record. Quickly, the lottery directors and their elected bosses recognized that this was not enough.

To the rescue came the public relations consultants, who saw the problem as an opportunity not just to set the record straight, but to do a great deal more. This was a chance to glorify the lottery, not just merely legitimize it. So a whole new generation of lottery advertising was launched. It was heavy on visuals of the elderly and the young, with a strong taint of exploitation of the handicapped who got paraded in front of the cameras to convey the message that the lottery is not just okay, but it is absolutely blessed in its beneficence to the downtrodden and needy. The blind, the deaf, the sick, and the lame all became camera fodder, there for us to see alongside the lottery director, or more likely the governor, who conveys the public service announcement that the lottery is helping all these poor unfortunates. One is forced to conclude that if using the elderly and the handicapped to glorify the most regressive form of taxation is acceptable, then these ads are not only successful, but also in the best of taste.

The final aspect of the massive advertising campaigns that warrants comment is what might be described as the "Heisenberg effect" on lottery operations. A short explanation may be in order. Werner Heisenberg, a physicist best known for his work in quantum physics, recognized the impossibility of ever making a totally objective observation. Since the apparatus with which one makes the observation (whether it be the eye, ear, camera, or electronic sensor) is subject to molecular change itself as the observation is being made, the phenomenon is always subject to some degree of change both in terms of what is being observed and on the part of the observer as well. There is no such thing, therefore, as a completely unaffected recording of anything. The watcher is changing just as the thing being watched is changing. As most scientists would put it: "The experimenter becomes an integral part of the experiment." Hopefully, the point becomes clear if we make the operation of the lotteries the thing that is to be observed.

Who, on this enlarged metaphoric scale, are the observers? The institution that we have selected in our pluralistic and open society to be our trusted observer is the media. It was previously mentioned in this work that we might expect, in the year 1988, almost $200,000,000 to be pumped into the economy by way of promotions of state-run lotteries. The vast majority of these funds will find their way into the bottom lines of radio stations, newspaper publishing companies, and television networks. Doesn't this enormous amount of money change, if not distort, the observations being made of the lottery operations? Isn't it the media that will be the beneficiary of the introduction of a new game with its budget for additional advertising? Isn't it the media that is inextricably intertwined with the lotteries' success or failure?

Lottery advertising is not the first instance in which the media has had to consider the ethical problems involved in balancing protection of the First Amendment freedoms with the protection of the public from harmful products. The media, in other words, are not on virgin territory; they previously have heard the seductive siren's song from the tobacco and liquor industries. How have they protected their integrity in the past? Not credibly, nor well. Take a look at the experience of tobacco advertising. For twenty-five years, we have had the categorical and unequivocal warnings of the nation's surgeons general that cigarette smoking, beyond the possibility of a doubt, is dangerous and deadly. Recently, the warnings from that office have been expanded to include not only the danger to the smoker but to those around him. The media dutifully has responded by writing editorials calling for everything from tougher warnings on the packaging to the elimination of agricultural subsidies for tobacco farmers to the outlawing of smoking in public places.

The editorial writers and their publishers know that about one out of every twenty-five readers gets to the editorial page after avidly reading the sports, comics, and even sometimes the news. In the meantime, the same edition that has carried the scathing editorial jeremiad against smoking may well contain extensive, as well as expensive, ads for various brands of cigarettes. How expensive, you ask? The most recent report available from the Federal Trade Commission says that the tobacco industry spent about $2.5 billion in just one year advertising and promoting its wares. Newspapers alone got about $200 million of that budget, and magazines got nearly double that amount. In addition, millions went to outdoor advertising on billboards. The largest owner of billboards also happens to be the owner of a huge newspaper chain.

This is not to say that the newspaper people have ignored the moral dilemma. They are very aware of the awkward position in which they find themselves. However, being conscious of the problem has had little or no effect on their behavior. The American Newspaper Publishers Association rationalizes itself out of the quandary by arguing that they carry cigarette ads not for the money but to advance the principle of free speech. No distinction, of course, is made between commercial free speech and what we all understand to be free speech as it applies to the traditional areas of politics, religion, philosophy, and science. Commercial speech falls into a separate category, and neither the courts nor the public consider the sacred rights of free speech abridged by restrictions on certain types of purely commercial advertising. Many newspapers already selectively draw the line.

Richard Harwood, the ombudsman for the Washington *Post* recently pointed out that his paper will not run ads for the sale of handguns which, while outlawed in the District of Columbia, are perfectly legal in the Virginia and Maryland sections of the paper's circulation. Harwood also said that, "...such constraints on commercial speech, it is said, are applied very selectively because if the paper got into the business of banning advertisements for all harmful products, there would be no end to it." He went on to cite some examples such as liquor, red meat, automobiles, and even the armed forces recruiting efforts, all of which could be harmful to your health. Finally, he cited as the justification for papers continuing to run ads for virtually anything, the "slippery slope" argument. This is a term normally used in the teaching of constitutional law. It is a shorthand way of explaining the reason why courts don't get involved in certain issues. The logic is that a specific issue is a slippery slope, and once you set foot on it, there is no telling where you stop.

The print media can use this logic as well, and thereby feel comfortable saying that if it is a good enough reason to justify nonintervention by the Supreme Court, then it is certainly a strong enough reason to support their policy of nondiscrimination in accepting advertising dollars from anyone who can pay the price. Harwood, to his credit, doesn't buy into this sophistry and concludes that the *Post* should abandon it as well. For him the choice is clear: If you are going to adopt an editorial policy against tobacco products, then don't run their ads. On the other hand, if you take their money, stop sermonizing about the product that you are helping to sell.

This suggested standard is a great deal more defensible than the obvious hypocrisy of defending, without exception, unbridled commercial speech. Likewise, this standard makes more sense than reliance on the pedagogy of the slippery-slope argument.

Even public broadcasting stations are not insulated from the influence of lottery advertising. The example that comes so readily to mind is New Jersey Public Broadcasting, which has been struggling to bring its viewers quality programs for almost twenty years. Their budget has always been tight, and often subject to heated debates in the legislative appropriations process. They have, like all other noncommercial networks, run an annual beg-a-thon, groveling for pledges to keep them on the air. What a welcome relief for those people, so deeply committed to their mission, to know that a promotional fee will be paid by the state's lottery operation for the privilege of drawing the number on the live broadcast each evening. The irony of this is that year after year, without fail and without exception, the lottery drawing commands the largest audience of any show. Nothing, in fact, is even in the running. The opera, concerts, nature shows, science shows, classic movies, the state news—nothing can command even half the audience that tunes in religiously to find out what the daily numbers are. Yet, a promotional fee is paid, and even more eagerly accepted. Of course, what it is, in reality, is a subsidy given to the public network to help them get by without the necessity for more tax dollars. It may, perhaps, also be a peace token, offered to any crusading reporters for the network who might have the passing thought that the lotteries would be an interesting change of pace after all the other routine budget stories. People don't, as a rule, bite the hand that feeds them. There are, of course, some exceptions, but they are just that.

This is only an example, and specifically has been chosen, since it illustrates that the magnifying glass rarely gets focused on the examiner's benefactors. If this occurs so demonstrably in the totally public sector, where independence and objectivity are considered to be sacrosanct, what can we expect in the mercantile atmosphere of the commercial media? Certainly, no promotional fee need be paid to the commercial media to carry the winning numbers. All of the media know that the availability of this pertinent information will attract audiences and readership. In fact, if they were cut off from opportunity of carrying this news, they would find themselves at a distinct disadvantage from their competitors. News of the numbers is an absolute staple for every editor in every media. Advertising rates for radio and television time slots adjacent to the numbers news are sold at a premium, because the audience is almost fanatical in its devotion. In the print medium, the ads for the lottery are often juxtaposed to the news of the previous day's winning numbers. The lottery is also promoted on the electronic medium, but never before the numbers are announced; always after the winning numbers are given. There is a reason for this, just as there is a reason for everything else that occurs in the world of lottery advertising. The best and most predictable purchasers of more tickets are, in fact, those who have won or come close to winning. Remember the words of Mr. Trahan about how difficult it is to keep the interest and loyalty of those who don't win. That people have certain expectations, and when they are frustrated it is greater challenge to maintain product sales. What, of course, could readily be inferred from all this is that there is no problem whatsoever to keep up the interest and loyalty of those who are lucky enough to win. Have you ever read a story or seen an interview where the winner has said, "Well, that is the last ticket I'll ever buy"? The opposite is what is true and is borne out by the reports of interviews with thousands of winners in various states. They all indicate that their allegiance is stronger than ever and that, in fact, in the cases where the win resulted in a few hundred dollars as opposed to a substantial jackpot, the interviewees usually intended to plow back the lion's share of their "hit" into more lottery tickets.

In conclusion, it can be said that there is enormous room for improvement in the advertising policies of the lotteries. The practices of the media must be left to their own evaluation and introspection, but it is difficult to quarrel with the attitude expressed by Mr. Harwood. The media, as an acknowledged watchdog of our institutions, should not succumb to the same type of double standard that they normally would be expected to expose. In the interim, the media runs a substantial risk of having both their credibility and objectivity called into serious question by careful and thoughtful observers of the interplay between advertising and editorial policy. It is a problem that can only be identified by observers. In a free society, such as ours, the problem can only be resolved by the standards that a free press sets for itself.

On the other hand, the troublesome policies of the lottery operations can be reformed. The suggested changes are outlined in chapter 12. As will be seen, such reforms do not run afoul of the First Amendment, nor are they so restrictive as to cripple the success of the lotteries. The proposed reforms do, however, require the resolve to alter business-as-usual attitudes, and the resolve to adhere to the basic ethical precepts that were promised to be honored at the outset of the lottery phenomena.

PART III

9

Tax Reform: Toward a Less Regressive Lottery

The lottery's implied tax is regressive because of the states' inordinately high take-out rate, and because those who can least afford it pay the highest proportional share.

Here are three ways to combat this:

1. Reduce the implied tax rate by increasing the payout share;
2. Broaden the taxpayer base with a special effort to bring in high-earning players and reduce the number of low income ones; and
3. Establish a rebate or credit program to lessen the regressive impact of the lotteries.

We saw in chapter 4 that lotteries in the United States are regressive. They don't have to be, and, in fact, are not that way in other places in the world where the lottery is played legally. You'll recall that for those who never win, the effective tax rate is 100 percent. The total take-out, including operating expenses, averages 50 percent. However the take-out or tax is measured, the lotteries, measured as a tax, have the highest excise rate of all existing taxes in the United States.

Because of the political imperatives discussed earlier, it is understandable that governments are extremely reluctant to abandon—or even diminish—efforts to extract maximum returns from their lottery operations. Yet, there is no reason to hope that gradually increasing concern over the dangers in the way lotteries raise money eventually may outweigh the benefits of the programs financed by these revenues.

Over the past two decades we occasionally have witnessed one state or another dramatically break away from the pack, but the breakaway has always been in the form of a new technological application of computers, or the introduction of a new type of game, such as lotto. No state has yet to consider marketing a game, old or new, with basically a higher pay-out rate for the players. Of course, such an arrangement is possible; in fact, larger overall pay-outs and more prizes at various levels are the practice in many other countries. Therefore, the suggestion that states lower their implied tax and raise their pay-outs comes as nothing revolutionary, only as something untried in the United States in modern times.

It isn't as though the states weren't aware of what the rest of the world was doing. The states willfully chose from the very outset to reach for the limits of what the public would tolerate. As far back as 1969, New Jersey, before implementing its lottery, took the time to study the operations in other coun-tries, but chose not to emulate them. However, in their report, the commission studying the prospect of a lottery did include a section that dealt with the probability of winning in various countries and states.

In Mexico, the probability of winning was very high, running between 21 and 31 percent. In France, the odds dropped to 25 percent, or one chance in four. In Puerto Rico, the odds were reported as being 15 to 16 percent. These odds are not very high, but they are remarkable when they are compared to the odds in the New York lottery. In this study, the odds of winning any prize in the New York lottery were reported to be only 0.12 percent. In New Hampshire, the probability was only slightly higher at 2.4 percent. With the low odds of winning in New York, no wonder only 30 percent of all wagered dollars were paid out in prizes.

Conversely, in France and Mexico, where the odds of winning were so much better, 66 percent of all the funds bet went back to the players in the form of prizes.

New Jersey and all the other states that have opted for lotteries knew these facts, but they also knew that a populace deprived of a legal mechanism for gambling for three generations would tolerate high odds and low probabilities of winning.

The odds haven't improved much over the years, and there is some fear that the American experience may, by example, be influencing many of the other lottery-playing countries, who look enviously at the large profits being real-ized here. American lotteries are not generous, but they are highly profitable. What would happen if American lotteries adopted more generous pay-outs? It might be worth the try from two public policy perspectives.

First, the lottery, as a tax, would be made less regressive, and second, such action would broaden the market, possibly generating more revenue. By lowering their take-outs and increasing their pay-outs, states indeed might broaden the market in the way that everyone, including the lottery directors themselves, agrees it should be broadened, by bringing more players in at the top of the income scale. The educated and the affluent see a good deal when it presents itself.

This potential effect should be tested by running test games with proper advertising and promotion indicating that the pay-outs will be higher and the chances of winning better. More people who appreciate the odds may be willing to take a chance given the proposition that a better and fairer deal is being offered. The broadening of the market is impossible, however, unless the states do substantially more than just change the odds. The states also must follow through with a bona fide commitment to change both their marketing and advertising practices.

The third alternative for potential reduction of the lotteries' regressivity is rebates and/or credits. For example, programs such as homestead rebates, senior citizen rebates, veterans rebates, and circuit breakers are used by many states to lessen the impact of property taxes. Implicit in these programs is the financial need or hardship of the taxpayer.

Other programs rebate, directly or indirectly, some portion of other major broad-base taxes; i.e., sales taxes and income taxes. Three taxes—sales, income, and property—are commonly factored into the final taxpayer formula to ensure that those with lower incomes are not oppressed.

This is done by allowing taxpayers to deduct from their state income tax returns the amount that they pay in local property tax, and/or to deduct a certain amount for assumed sales tax payments. An alternative to this is a provision for a sales tax credit which is deducted from the bottom line of what is owed in state income taxes. Some states go even further, allowing lower income earners to deduct even more than is allowed for higher income earners. Dozens of alternatives to the rebating approach are presently in effect in the various states.

Circuit breaking is a somewhat more complex concept, but its ultimate effect is to ensure that no lower income taxpayer pays more than a fixed percentage of disposable income in combined income, sales, and/or property taxes. In other words, if the circuit breaker is set at 10 percent, and a citizen's property taxes on his home combined with his income tax obligation is greater than the limit of that 10 percent, no more can be collected. If more tax has already been collected or withhheld, the taxpayer is entitled to a rebate for the amount paid over the 10 percent.

Exemptions, rebates, deductions, credits, and circuit breakers serve the same purpose. They reduce regressivity in the overall tax structure. But is there any way to reduce regressivity as it applies to the lottery?

Traditionally, the various federal and state income tax codes have reflected little, if any, sympathy for the gambler. Ironically, most tax codes have provided much greater protection for professional gamblers than for amateurs. Historically, the rule has been that a taxpayer may deduct gaming losses of every kind, but only to the extent that such losses offset reported winnings. Few, however, took advantage of this provision. Professional gamblers with high winnings scrupulously documented their losses. Professional gamblers knew how to take advantage of the tax system. At the race track, large bets are rarely made in one lump sum, but in multiple smaller bets so that no one ticket will have a pay-off large enough to trigger federal or state withholding requirements. To further reduce exposure, knowledgeable gamblers cash winning tickets on separate occasions or at separate windows.

Lastly, professional gamblers cherish what the rest of us discard—losing tickets. The professionals squirrel away these otherwise worthless slips of paper just in case they have more reported winners than they expected. There are people at the race tracks who surreptitiously go around picking up losing tickets that have been discarded. This, by the way, is illegal, but there is a thriving market in the sale of losing tickets to those who need the proof of gambling loses to offset winnings that they are forced to report.

All of this is set out to show that the really serious gamblers have found creative ways of handling federal and state income taxes. The average lottery player is not a professional gambler. He is someone with dreams rather than schemes. So deductions and set-offs for losses are extremely unusual, if not nonexistent, for those who play the lottery.

Two threshold questions arise from this. First, do lottery players warrant any special consideration in the tax codes? Second, can the regressive effects of the implied lottery tax be reduced by using rebates or credits?

The answer to the first question depends on whether we wish to adhere to the old-fashioned mentality that said all gambling is sinful, and, therefore, should be highly taxed. That mentality leaves a little to be desired when we consider that lottery betting is no longer a sin, but is now considered as a virtue by the treasury office. Those who cling to puritanical notions regarding wagering might consider that the excise tax on liquor rarely exceeds 20 percent, and even cigarette taxes run slightly more than 20 percent range. These are moderate when compared to the lottery tax.

Lottery sales are a substantial additional tax obligation, voluntary or otherwise, for states to levy from the poor without having some qualms. Efforts at tax reform have been properly aimed most often at this very group of low-income earners. Most states address tax relief efforts at middle-income families as well, the same groups that are spending large amounts on the lottery games. Why structure tax policy on the basis of ability to pay if many of the reform efforts are effectively negated for many by the implied lottery tax?

The answer to the question of rebates and credits as devices to lessen the regressive effects of lotteries' implied tax is not likely. For one thing, rebates or credits would be counterproductive in that they would encourage more gambling. Worse, credits would reward the gambler, and thereby deny equal treatment to the industrious and prudent. The principle, as well as the practical problem, in attempting to reduce regressivity in this manner is that the administration of any type of rebate or credit program would be extraordinarily cumbersome and difficult.

I propose a method by which the worst aspects of the regressivity that are associated with the lottery operations could be lessened, without unduly rewarding individual gamblers. Easy to administer, my solution is to refund *a portion* of the implied tax, not to individuals (whose lottery-ticket purchases may or may not correspond to their income-tax level), but to the communities and programs within the communities (where the tickets are purchased). Using lottery revenue to finance socially beneficial programs that most directly help the poor—the class that can least afford to play the low-odds lottery—is an indirect, but, I believe, useful means of restoring a portion of what the state extracts to those most in need. This proposal will be spelled out in detail. But, first, it is useful to reexamine how most of the states operate.

There presently exists in no state a direct correlation between the lottery purchases and the beneficiaries of that implied tax. States channel their lottery profits into programs that generally enjoy widespread acceptance. That will be not only politically palatable, but will add to the general perception that the lotteries are good and salutary operations that provide needed funds for worthwhile purposes. In New Jersey, for instance, television commercials feature the governor surrounded by happy children telling us how the lottery has helped the State School for the Deaf. In his closing line, the governor says: "The lottery, can you imagine our state without it?"

A Maryland lottery print ad of the early 1980s featured the picture of a black teenaged girl who was blind. The ad revealed how much the state was doing to support better education for the blind, pointing out that the lottery helped the general fund. The written message was one thing, but the visual told a more direct story—the lottery helps poor, unfortunate, blind minority children.

The real message of these two ads and others using the same technique is that the lottery is socially acceptable, and, by inference, virtually sacrosanct. It would appear that the goal of these ads is to make the lottery, as tax policy, immune from criticism. This effective and sophisticated advertising is common in every state. It is often justified in the name of open government—telling the people where their money is going.

Even more insidious is the political "shell game" by which voters are led to believe that lottery money dedicated for a purpose is going to be spent *in addition* to tax revenues already earmarked for that same purpose. This is often not the case. In California, for example, the lottery was promoted as a supplement to the state's education budget, intended to fund special programs which would not ordinarily be funded. Instead, according to California's Superintendent of Public Instruction Bill Honig, budget cuts to education wipe out the additional funds brought in by the lottery. In an article in the Miami *Herald* in November 1988 he says, "We call it 'the sting.' In the front door they're bringing in the money. In the back, they're taking it away." California's education budget dropped from 38.6 percent of the state's budget in 1986 to 37.3 percent in 1988—a loss of almost $500 million. "If you're going to advertise 'Schools win too,' " says Honig, "you should put a tag line—'not very much.' " In an effort to remedy this, California placed on its ballot in 1988 a proposition to guarantee the schools a base level of funding, calculated as a fixed percentage of the state budget.

The same misleading advertising is a problem in Illinois, too. Michael Belletire, Associate Superintendent for Finance and Administration for the Illinois State Board of Education, says, in the same Miami *Herald* article, that advertising in Illinois creates the perception that the purchase of a lottery ticket expands the money available for education. "We don't turn around and say, 'Buy an automobile or a TV set—the sale tax supports schools,' but it's the same analogy."

Such games are played easily with earmarked funds by experienced budget officials. Some experts suggest that earmarking lottery funds for purposes that already receive large amounts of money, such as education, is an invitation to creating a shell game. Just as Superintendent Honig says, what basically happens in this game is that lottery revenues are brought in the front door, while other money, which would have been appropriated anyway, is secreted out the back door to be applied somewhere else within the state's budget. Careful scrutiny of a state budget document is a powerful soporific, so most of the subtle internal shifting of funds is rarely detected.

It would appear, then, that dedicated lottery revenues are often cushions which allow budget planners to manipulate appropriations as may be expedient, while the public is led to believe its purchase of tickets (or tolerance for public gaming) is justified on grounds that the needy or misfortunate benefit, when, in fact, the lottery revenues are marginal contributors to such worthy enterprises. How could this happen, and, more importantly, how can it be corrected?

The answer may be found in a reform which I advocate that would send lottery revenues back to the municipalities in proportion to the tickets sold in those municipalities. Further, statutory provisions should be adopted to ensure the municipalities use the funds for specific programs to benefit those in need, thus preventing municipal leaders from succumbing to the same temptations which presently lure state officials—namely, using lottery income to defray general government expenses that are presently financed by more conventional taxes.

Lottery proponents argue many wagered dollars stimulate local economies through expenditures on advertising and retail sales commissions. However, very few people living in the ghettos and barrios own television networks or newspaper chains. Likewise, a majority of lottery ticket outlets in the country are owned by corporations. Even independently owned outlets are seldom, if ever, owned by anyone in the low-income category. Lottery dollars follow a one-way street out of the poorest neighborhoods, and few, if any, of these dollars ever find their way back into the areas from whence they came.

I propose a plan that would statutorily mandate at least 25 percent of the lottery tax be returned to those areas from which it was extracted.

The sales figures tell a story. The games are, and remain, urban games. Revenue sharing is the simplest and fairest way of redirecting the benefits of the dollars collected back to the tax base that generated those dollars to begin with.

Massachusetts has already moved in the right direction. All of the proceeds of their popular lottery operation go to the cities and towns of the state. In a substantial way, Massachusetts has effectively reduced the overall regressivity of its lottery. Net proceeds are distributed on a formula that divides the population of each community into the total property tax base of the municipality. Using this method, towns with fewer local resources receive more, and wealthier towns get less. The buyers of lottery tickets there have the chance of seeing their money coming back into their communities. This also contributes to lowering local levies in towns with smaller property-tax bases. As tax policy, Massachusetts' system of distribution is a progressive model.

Massachusetts has demonstrated one excellent approach to providing for more equitable distribution of lottery revenues. States interested in eliminating, or at least abating, the regressive aspect of their lottery tax would do well to follow the Massachusetts example.

10

Budget Process Reform:
Pulling in the States' Necks

In the previous chapter, three ways of reducing regressivity of lottery taxes were proposed:

1. Lowering the tax rate or take-out from the high rates, and capping the implied tax at a maximum of 32 percent. This would increase the pay-out and allow more people to win.
2. Broadening the spectrum of participants by targeting more lottery marketing, promotion, and advertising at the wealthy.
3. Guaranteeing that the communities which support the lottery are allowed to participate in its success—at least to some degree—by rebating to the communities a minimum of 25 percent of the net proceeds from the sales of tickets that originate in those communities; or states could follow the more ambitious model of Massachusetts.

Ameliorating the effects of regressive taxation is a necessary reform, as is the elimination of exploitative promotion, abusive marketing, and questionable advertising. But these are merely symptoms of a larger problem that must be addressed—a problem that is fundamental to the fiscal policy of the states themselves.

The root problem is the budget process itself that inexorably drives the lottery system to seek more revenue. The pressure to submit a balanced state budget is enormous, but the risks for a state in ignoring potential consequences for the benefit of temporarily balancing a budget are very serious.

States spend money through an appropriations process that anticipates funds before they are actually collected. Increasing revenue projections gives rise to increased expectations. But projected lottery receipts are merely expectations.

Other state revenues, such as income taxes or sales taxes, are subject to more accurate analysis. Traditional taxes have long-charted histories, and are subject to national trends that are picked up rather quickly on the seismographs of economists. However, aberrations in lotteries are subject to trends that are less easily detected.

When state revenues fall short, governors and legislators are confronted with the onerous and unhappy choice of cutting programs or raising taxes. The lottery business provides a seductive alternative that may free decision-makers from these politically unpalatable choices. By fattening up lottery projections, elected state officials are allowed to stave off, for perhaps another year, the unpleasant task of confronting reality. On the one hand, the manipulation of lottery revenue estimates provides an escape hatch for politicians; on the other hand, this manipulation sends a clear signal to lottery directors that they are being given tacit approval, if not actual encouragement, to boost sales by virtually any means.

The key to removing undue pressures on lottery systems—pressures which by their nature lead to abuses described herein—is to relieve the lottery system of meeting unrealistic revenue expectations. The reform I propose would prohibit the appropriation of lottery receipts not, in fact, already collected. In other words, don't allow the states to gamble on lottery income. The shift in procedure would result in a major shift in the dynamics of the lottery operations. As constituted in all states presently, the system gives rise to revenue expectations that politicians too easily treat as guarantees. No politician wants to be wrong. No budget official wants to be wrong. But if lottery revenues flatten, pressures increase to do something to prove that they were not wrong.

It is a simple matter to deny responsibility if sales tax or income tax receipts drop below projections. "The president blew it," or "Congress is out of control," or "the folks on Wall Street are playing a game with the economy," or "the Japanese are undermining our economy." There are dozens of excuses and dozens of potential scapegoats for downturns in the economy. But should the lottery revenues fall short, it is more difficult to assign blame.

One such shortfall was addressed recently in Michigan. The law in that state provides that lottery officials must submit projected revenues not just one year but two full years in advance. In 1985, the budget officials, flushed with the apparent success of the recently introduced lotto game, projected net lottery revenues for fiscal year 1987 to be $489.6 million. But the projected income was far too optimistic, and there was an $82.5 million shortfall. Because lottery revenue in Michigan is committed by statute to school aid funds, the shortfall rested directly on education. The flushes turned to blushes on the faces of budget officials, and Governor James Blanchard responded by appointing a fourteen-member Task Force to find out what went wrong, and how to correct it. Many of the recommendations found in their final report, released in March 1988, mirror, to some extent, reforms suggested in this treatise. Some of the other recommendations confirm predictions this work makes as to future marketing and advertising trends.

Among their recommendations were the slight increase in the pay-out to stimulate sales. Another recommendation was that a careful analysis of erosion in agents' sales be undertaken before resorting to further expansion of terminals.

As to those recommendations that incorporate more aggressive marketing and promotion techniques, the Michigan report proposed:

1. Allowing the licensing of sales kiosks in shopping-center malls (see chapter 7).
2. Increasing subscription marketing to cut out agent commissions (see chapter 7).
3. Launching a public relations campaign to improve public awareness that the funds are essential for educational purposes (see chapters 8 and 9).

The task force did not confront the real cause of the problem in Michigan. The lottery didn't fail the people of Michigan; rather, it was state officials who overestimated revenues, and gave the people delusions of fiscal well-being.

Some budget officials, lottery officials, and particularly legislators, who don't want either to cut programs or to raise taxes, may be willing to try anything to get more money out of the lottery. These improper pressures will disappear once the process is changed to provide that only monies already received may be appropriated. This reform is more sensible and more important than all of the other recommendations in the Michigan report.

Paul Dworin wrote in the April 1988 edition of his *Gaming and Wagering Business,* "But we think the task force missed an opportunity for more positive change by overlooking the real significance of the shortfall: *Lottery revenues are impossible to predict with any real exactitude and, as such, should be appropriated only after they are actually received by the state treasury."* (emphasis added)

Lottery revenues are different—different in their origins; different in their predictability; different in their vulnerability to political manipulation. Therefore, lottery receipts should be treated differently, and spent only after they are actually collected by the treasurers' offices.

11

Marketing Reform

Large-scale gambling lotteries have only become practical since the popularization of the Arabic number system by Leonardo Fibonacci, who was also known as Leonardo of Pisa and who, in 1202, published his most famous work, *Liber Abaci (Book of the Abacus)* which introduced the concept of Arabic numerals to western civilization. (Actual credit for the introduction of Arabic numerals to the West belongs to Adelard of Bath, who was the tutor of the young Henry II of England. But Adelard apparently did not make much of an impression, since his student kept his name.) Even more important than the numerals themselves was the concept of "zero," which makes possible modern mathematics. It might be possible to run a very small lottery using "C's," "L's," "M's," and "V's," but it would be awkward to attempt to run a lottery on a modern computer network if Roman numerals were still the standard. The popular science writer Isaac Asimov, commenting on Fibonacci's contribution, said, "Since Arabic numerals are only about a trillion times as useful as Roman numerals, it took a mere couple of centuries to convince European merchants to make the change."

There still are small cliques of devoted Leonardo fans, and even a British journal called the *Fibonacci Quarterly*, which focuses on esoteric conundrums in keeping with a grand tradition started by Fibonacci himself to demonstrate the superiority of his new method.

The most famous of his math problems, and the one that has given rise to an idiom that is still current today, involved "multiplying like rabbits." The problem as originally posed was: How many rabbits can be produced from a single pair in a year, if every month each pair begets a new pair, which from the second month on become productive, and no deaths occur? The answer is 144, but how many will there be at the end of three years? This is a very important question and the answer, since it involved the first demonstration of a mathematical progression, was of even greater significance. Without demonstrating the entire sequence, suffice it to say that at the end of the third year there are about 15 million rabbits.

Since the first pair of "sweepstakes" outlets were opened, at the race track windows in New Hampshire in 1964, we have witnessed lottery sales locations multiplying like Fibonacci's rabbits. The hypothetical rabbits could continue to replicate themselves into infinity, but after about ten years, they would have consumed all the food in the entire world, thereby exterminating every other species. There is a lesson to be learned from all this.

The proliferation of lottery outlets, the resources they consume, and the competition they destroy, are subjects worthy of serious reflection.

From its humble beginnings in New Hampshire, the lotteries have grown into an enormous industry. In less than twenty years, over $100 billion worth of lottery tickets have been sold. Annual gross sales for 1988 alone are projected to $15 billion or more. These sales will be transacted at 80,000 outlets throughout the United States.

Yet this industry's financial future is cloudy. Most of the problems are presently internal, but how the industry responds could dictate whether or not the public will feel the brunt of these difficulties in future years. Agents, who may be indispensable for the present, are facing obsolescence as the states, in an effort to cut overhead, design systems that will eliminate them. Increased expenditures for older lotteries have leveled out in all but a few states. The value of adding additional terminals also seems to have peaked for the more established lotteries such as Connecticut's and New Hampshire's, while growth continues mostly in states where the lottery is less than ten years old. Wherever the lottery has been in existence for any appreciable length of time the operation's growth and growth potential have flattened.

Jim Hosker, director of the Massachusetts Lottery, projects a statewide ratio of one terminal for every 1,250 people. He was already close to that goal in 1987 when he told *Gaming and Wagering Business* magazine that "the most important thing when terminals are installed is to measure the effect on total business. Without question, there is a saturation point in a given city or town where the only thing a new terminal will do is result in moving the business around within the jurisdiction, with the total net revenue not increasing. If the total for that city or town is not increasing with the installation of new terminals, then the process should be stopped." The president of the British Columbia Lottery, Guy Simonis, was more straightforward. "Terminal density is governed by what the traffic will bear," he said.

The marketing value of increasing lottery ticket outlets appears to have become marginal in states with systems that are "mature," i.e., ten or more years old. The present challenge to these older operations is how to increase sales now that terminal saturation has been reached and the addition of any new outlet only results in taking business away from existing outlets. Some state systems are responding to this challenge with new—and potentially dangerous —marketing techniques.

These new sales efforts would concentrate on direct sales from the states' offices to the players, cutting out the commissions now received by the agents, and rely on telecommunications and computer technology. The final element would be to keep players' money on deposit to allow them to place their bets by phone, using their state code, thus freeing them from the nuisance of keeping records. This apparent convenience is really just another way of allowing the state to enhance lottery by earning interest on the players' money.

An alternative to adding outlets as a means of increasing sales is marketing by mail. For a number of years, some states have been trying to market tickets directly by mail, thereby cutting the need for agents, but also broadening their market to those who are geographically isolated. Farmers, students, military personnel on active duty, and shut-ins constitute this potential mail-order market. Direct sales by mail have already raised some unique problems. In Illinois, an inmate at the Pontiac Correctional Center wrote to the state lottery office asking for an application to play by mail. The applicant, who is serving a life sentence for murder, was told to get the consent of the state's Department of Corrections. The assistant warden said no, and the inmate filed a federal lawsuit. The case is pending.

Lottery experts and observers acknowledge that marketing by mail has not experienced the success that was envisioned; but in all fairness, efforts to promote purchase by mail have not been very intense, and states have been focusing on other alternatives.

Michigan produced a creative variation on a time-tested marketing ploy by allowing workers to buy tickets at work through payroll deductions.

Since 1985, New Hampshire has solicited out-of-state subscriptions by permitting phone purchases. Callers are able to charge the $55 fee for participation in New Hampshire's 52 Megabuck drawings on their credit cards. The sale of tickets in this manner by a small state such as New Hampshire may appear innocuous for the moment, but if this is the wave of the future, we might want to make some policy judgment, before the practice spreads. Every lottery is developing long-range marketing plans. How far advanced are some of these plans? Consider this remark of David Clark, president of Loto-Quebec, "I have no idea what our network's size will be at maturity. The maximum limit is being in every home. I think that is where we'll be in the year 2000."

I advocate a ban on lottery betting by phone. Phone betting is the ultimate in oversaturation; it is aimed at the impulsive behavior. Nothing intervenes to deter or even chill the compulsive bettor. A wager could be made any time, day or night, by phone. There would be no chance for a little reflection on the way to the ticket counter. Competing needs are not even present. The player in the supermarket or at the newsstand confronts the choice of buying more food or a magazine. Forced to buy at an outlet, the prospective player has the opportunity to "cool off," as they say in gambling parlance. Cooling off is the chance to assess what your real financial situation is, and to measure what you really can afford to bet. Cooling off doesn't help the compulsive gambler who is in a perpetual fever, but the normal player only has the fever come upon him at intervals. There is also the problem of restricting sales to minors and inebriates.

The problems that surfaced almost immediately after commercial "party lines" were introduced in the spring of 1988 offer some insight in to the dangers we court if we adopt bet-by-phone lotteries. This new service involves dialing a number, which puts the caller in touch with a party line of like-minded people. The abuses became evident within the first few months of operation. Subscribers complained that they were promised early warnings if their monthly expenditures exceeded either $100 or $200; but warnings never came, and bills soon mounted into the thousands of dollars. How did these people allow their bills to get so high? The reasons given were the typical ones. No one warned them that the costs were getting out of hand. But usually it was just that the compulsive talkers just could not help themselves. It was so easy to become engrossed in conversation and lose track of how much was being spent. One 18-year-old ran up $4000 on his parents' phone bill in the course of just one month. If people became addicted to mere conversation so easily, what projections can we make about addiction to gambling by phone?

The social and behavioral problems present in electronic gambling, and particularly betting by phone, apply to automated ticket sales. Neither vending machines nor video lottery devices can monitor ticket buyers. The placement of additional machines, of course, constitutes saturation. Like phone sales, video games and ticket vending machines encourage impulse gambling and their prohibition might well be properly considered.

Electronic marketing poses another danger. There are basically two ways to design systems for the sale of lottery tickets. The first is a system that is labor-intensive, and the second is capital-intensive. All lotteries presently operating in North America still rely heavily on the use of people to operate the on-line terminals, and to this extent must be considered labor-intensive. Everything in the lottery operations, before and after the transaction at the point of sale, is capital-intensive, requiring complex and expensive computer networking as opposed to physical labor. The trend, however, is to rely more and more on machines and less on human labor. The practice in other countries has been to keep the lottery operations labor-intensive. Some countries have gone so far as to resist efforts to mechanize their systems to avoid eliminating jobs.

Vending tickets on the street is still common in many Latin American countries, where lotteries exist, in part, as a social welfare mechanism, putting the handicapped to work. In these countries, it is customary to ensure tickets are sold by those who might otherwise not be self-supporting. The creation of jobs and the consequent dignity of self-sufficiency are viewed as positive objectives, and measured on an equal scale with the revenue generated for the government. The lottery operations in other countries have not permitted cost-effectiveness to become the sole criteria of success, to the exclusion of all other social values.

In North America, retail vendors tend to be successful convenience-store chains, liquor dealers, and large supermarket operations. Here, it is strictly business, with no room left to accommodate unprofitable social values. Lottery directors in the United States contend they are running a profit-oriented enterprise, and they are undoubtedly correct. That doesn't mean that high return and sensitivity to social cocerns are totally incompatible. Ideas can be implemented to improve the existing sales networks and, at the same time, advance social concerns which almost everyone recognizes to be valid. For example, in those states where supermarket chains are the largest distributors, it makes sense to mandate that they coordinate their hiring with the state's unemployment offices and job-training programs as a condition to being given the franchise to sell lottery tickets. When $200 million worth of advertising contracts are awarded, the lottery directors can make sure they are awarded to companies with equal-opportunity employment policies. Ensuring job opportunities for the disadvantaged is the standard to which the states hold themselves; should not states require the same of those who sell lottery tickets in their name?

The second area of marketing reform requires that policymakers rethink fundamental assumptions about how lottery operations are presently structured. Revenue-motivated lottery offices should not be the same unit of government empowered to allocate outlets, or introduce new marketing methods. The potential for conflict is obvious. It is unrealistic to expect lottery offices to monitor, control, or discipline their agents. This problem alone demonstrates why the operational duties of the lottery systems should be separated from the agencies charged with regulating the lottery.

Regulation must be the province of an agency that is independent of the revenue-raising functions of the state governments. The structures in place could retain jurisdiction over the operation of the game itself. But the licensing and regulation of agents, the rules on franchises, and the standards of public convenience should be the responsibility of a separate agency—an agency whose mission and mandate is not revenue-raising, but enforcing regulations that ensure fairness, decency, and responsible practices. Until regulatory functions are divorced from the balance of the lottery operations, questionable marketing practices will prevail.

The third marketing reform flows naturally from the second. The new regulatory agency should be given specific standards to enforce. Such standards, to date, have been noticeably absent. The first standard to be adopted must be the limitation of the number and placement of terminals, to ensure that the ratio of outlets to population does not result in a pattern that exists in too many places. The ratio should be in direct correlation to the median income of the census tracts, which would reverse the present situation, where the number of outlets is in inverse ratio to the median income level of any given area.

In order to create a more acceptable ratio in urban centers, I advocate a regulatory policy that requires each vendor to demonstrate that the sale of lottery tickets is not the principal source of income to the enterprise. Outlets that have no other business but selling lottery tickets to the poor simply don't belong in business; yet a ride down urban streets reveals stores where the lottery is the only product advertised, and once inside the store, all that can be found are a few cartons of cigarettes, a cooler of soda, and, of course, the lottery terminal.

This reform does not eliminate the problem of saturation in the cities. There are a number of ways to address this ill. The first step in any remedial effort must be an immediate moratorium on new lottery retail outlets in communities that presently exceed the statewide average ratio of terminals to population. There are already more than needed in the poorest areas. An analysis must be made to determine the demographics of the markets to which each outlet is allegedly "convenient." The relevant figures to be studied would be the median incomes and the purchasing power indices applicable to the communities where the terminals are situated.

The reform I propose is the development of objective populace-to-terminal ratios. Statewide figures that indicate that ratio of terminals to population are misleading. They mask the fact that terminals are concentrated in the poorer areas. Even data on terminal distribution given by county or large municipalities can be misleading, and are used to conceal a pattern of saturation within pockets of poverty. The best statistical vehicles for measuring whether an abusive marketing pattern is in effect are the "tracts" established by the Federal Bureau of the Census. Whatever methodology is chosen, the goal remains the same, to remedy the lopsided terminal placement strategy that concentrates so heavily on marketing to the urban poor.

A final regulatory problem arises because agents appear to be free from scrutiny and immune to disciplinary action. An independent enforcement and regulatory agency could provide oversight currently neglected by lottery commissions solely concerned with revenues.

In summary, these three essential reforms are recommended:

1. Prohibit sales of lottery tickets via teleelectronic or automated machines.

2. Separate the functions of the lottery commissions to ensure that licensure and regulation are made by an agency that is independent of revenue-raising pressures and obligations.

3. Set definite standards and create finite limits on the number of retail outlets within a defined population, preferably using census tracts. If a given area is already saturated, steps should be taken to bring down the ratio to the state standard.

12

Advertising Reform

Perhaps someday in the future there will be a trivia question about what lottery ad was considered the most tasteless, or simply which one generated the most outrage. In the meantime the competition is still open, as some states apparently have been persuaded that hard-sell campaigns are necessary to promote sales.

Since its inception, lottery advertising has received more than mere protection. Because it is paid for by the state, it is presumed to be legitimate, and some of the most objectionable policies are tolerated because of states' sponsorship. Once again, the root of the problem is structural—the inherent conflict built into the operation of the lottery.

The state cannot exercise objectivity, much less ethical judgement, given the exigencies of the revenue-raising obligations that confront the lottery decision-makers. The decisionmaking process is inexorably reduced to one and only one consideration—will it sell more tickets?

The problem is inextricably intertwined with the manner in which the states have structured lottery operations. Where there is no separation of duties there can be no separation of perspective. More than just good taste, or even truth in advertising, is at stake; the quality, tone, and content of advertising paid for by the state lottery operations reveal something about the nature of our society. If lottery advertising reflects contemporary community values, then it is a sad commentary on the narrowness of our mercantile lives.

We expect our government to protect our civil liberties. To that end, we all hope that the sovereign won't engage in improper censorship, or do anything that will have a chilling effect on our freedom to see and read what we choose. We have become conditioned to object to any type of prior restraint, even its most subtle variants. Our suspicions increase whenever anyone suggests that there is something that we can't read or hear. When we discuss the control of lottery advertising policies, we are not talking about the government interference with private enterprise, but suggesting a form of self-control.

Censorship is defined as the prior restraint of publication by the government of expression by private citizens. Regulating the advertising policies of the lotteries does not qualify as censorship. It must be considered mere self-restraint. This isn't semantic nit-picking, only the exercise of simple logic. The lottery advocates who insist that any restraint would violate the First Amendment simply don't understand the law. It is a graphic demonstration of the worst aspects of a double standard when the state, while controlling the advertising policies of private enterprise, contends it must have unbridled freedom to promote the sale of their unique product as they see fit.

While we Americans abhor censorship, we traditionally have insisted on institutionalizing the watchdog function with regard to the market place (for example, the FTC) and the communications industry (the FCC). Moreover, most states provide broad authority to their insurance and banking regulators to oversee advertising. Finally, in the private sector, the function of watchdog groups is not only tolerated, but encouraged. For example, the Children's Advertising Review Unit (CARU), an arm of the Better Business Bureau, recently jumped into the fray regarding television ads targeted at children. CARU recommends that all advertisers who target children follow the guidelines set forth by major television networks. These guidelines include recommendations, such as, "Must not overglamorize product," "No exhortative language such as 'Ask Mom to buy,' " "No celebrity endorsements," "Can't use 'only' or 'just' in regard to price." The object is to present a realistic picture of the toy or game so children or their parents won't be duped into buying a toy based on some advertiser's creativity.

While we're looking at advertising guidelines, we should review the state and media imposed restrictions on financial and insurance advertising. Accuracy and full disclosure are the watch words for the most part. Lending rates must be as advertised; and after applying for credit, the customer must be given a full truth-in-lending form prior to assuming any obligation. Recently, the insurance industry, especially that segment of it that does high-powered marketing to the elderly in the form of so-called "medigap" policies and "no rejection" life policies, came under intense scrutiny.

Prior to the imposition of moderate restraints, celebrities with soothing, credible voices were paid handsome fees to sell policies of dubious value. These ads often made grossly exaggerated claims as to the protection afforded by the insurance companies, marketing coverage to supplement Medicare, or "guaranteed acceptance" life insurance. Thankfully, state after state has insisted the ads be withdrawn. The companies, while maintaining their innocence, have had no stomach for battle with state insurance regulators or consumer activist groups. One example of what regulators considered to be particularly obnoxious is germane for its comparison to lottery advertising.

The National Benefit life insurance company used Dick Van Dyke to promote a policy to the middle-aged and elderly, a policy that, for less than $5 a month, would provide protection for the insured's loved ones. The policy was available regardless of the applicant's state of health. A person 65 years old could buy a maximum of $500 worth of protection for $4.95 a month. If the insured died within two years, the beneficiary didn't even get the full payoff of $500, but only a return of the premiums. At age 70, the maximum coverage is reduced to $350, but the premium remains the same. At age 71, having paid for six years, the policyholder has paid in $360 and stands to have his beneficiaries get back only $350. This is outrageous, but in its own strange way is probably much fairer than selling lottery tickets to the same age group. The naive policy-buyer has a better chance of collecting something than does the lottery player; at least his loved ones do.

This type of advertising is frowned upon because it is deceptive. The odds aren't spelled out in insurance advertising, but then again, they are rarely mentioned in lottery advertising. The difference is that the insurance ad has regulators screaming outrage, while their colleagues down the hall at the statehouse lay out the next lottery advertising campaign. The television ads which used celebrity spokespersons have been called as powerful as they are misleading. The lottery directors are blinded to how misleading and unfair their commercial message is.

It is unfair and misleading for one basic reason: Those who approve it are the same people who are responsible for the increase in the net profits of the operation. They just cannot exercise independent or objective judgement. The two functions of protecting the public from unfair advertising on the one hand, and selling the maximum amount of tickets on the other, are clearly incompatible.

I recommend that the power to decide on theme, tone, and content of advertising campaigns be placed in the hands of an agency separate and independent of the ticket-selling arm of the state government. Such a separation of duties would represent the accomplishment of three distinct goals: first, it will be a triumph of common sense; second, it will be a victory for good government; and finally, it will eliminate the double standard presently extant in the lottery operations.

An independent agency, therefore, would have the responsibility of insulating truly important policy decisions from the pressures of the state budget. Such an agency, created in each state, would be the final arbiter of community standards, and would have the final say on what should be permitted or proscribed in lottery advertising. In order to structure future discussions, I would personally suggest that there are at least five techniques or themes that are so offensive that little debate is warranted, and at the very minimum these five should go on any list of proscribed practices:

1. Any advertising that denigrates the work ethic should not be broadcast under the aegis of the state. We've simply spent too much effort in the opposite direction to tolerate such a counterproductive practice. Moreover, we are actively engaged in a struggle of international dimensions wherein productivity will be our most significant asset. In the final analysis, it comes down to the proposition of state-sponsored advertising being the major vehicle for the articulation of state policy. If, indeed, work-ethic bashing is not state policy, it should not be permitted to be projected as official policy. Since what appears in advertisements carrying the logo of the lottery commission can be assumed to be the official policy of the state, it should be filtered through a process that ensures that the message transmitted in the advertising campaign is the same as the message the governor would give at the state university's commencement ceremonies. An oversight agency for the lottery, answerable solely to the governor and not to the money-raising arm of the state government, can ensure that the theme of the lotteries' message is one that promotes the traditional values of the community rather than one that promotes the hope that you can win freedom from anything so menial as honest work.

2. The second standard that should be enforced is an agreement not to exploit the handicapped, the disabled, or the elderly to help promote the lottery. Messages that convey the impression that their quality of life will be diminished unless people continue to buy tickets is both false and misleading.

3. After work-ethic bashing and tearjerkers, the third most abusive technique is the false-hope or fantasy type of appeal. We have all heard or seen the messages that say that all our problems can be solved by purchasing more tickets. The fantasy is sometimes endorsed by a previous winner. This could be permissable if it were balanced by having other not-so-happy winners used in the advertising to tell how winning changed their lives for the worse. Additionally, such prolottery advertising could be balanced by commercials featuring people who fell victim to compulsive gambling on the lottery.

4. Let's have no more commercials that are intended to belittle or make light of the odds. It is bad enough to have advertising that ignores the odds; and it is not being recommended that anything as draconian as forcing the odds to be included in the advertisement become the standard. But, at the very minimum, we should expect that the states will not scoff at the laws of probability. After all, the states are continually putting out statistics, whether they be on the dangers of drunk driving or the virtues of education, that rely heavily on the audience accepting the laws of probability and being governed thereby. If we want people not to drink and drive because the statistics present a compelling message, why do we want people to laugh at the odds when it comes to gambling?

5. Remove the cynicism that is implicit in the present practices. This would mean a change in the scheduling of advertising promotion, as well as a

shift in other practices. In New Jersey, newspapers regularly run half-page and, occasionally, full-page ads on the second or third day of each month, instructing potential players how to wager on the latest lottery game. The timing isn't accidental. It is aimed at those who have just received their government checks on the first of the month. The other practices which need to be addressed are those that reflect an equal amount of cynicism, such as the heavy concentration on radio commercials, broadcast on stations whose audience consists of the urban poor. This is reverse elitism. Such practices are undoubtedly very productive from a sales-oriented perspective; but from another vantage point, the costs may prove excessive.

These five prohibitions will leave ample room for themes and techniques that are imaginative, and the creativity of the ad agencies has been only partially exercised. However, the tone and quality of the messages, and the clarity of official state policy, as articulated in its advertising programs, will be improved if these guidelines are enforced by an independent oversight agency.

Conclusion

We've taken a hard look at lotteries, and offered recommendations that are moderate and feasible. One might reasonably object that little mention has been made of the problem of compulsive gambling. I have tried to focus attention on reforms that are structural or institutional, and must leave improvements of human nature to those with more insight into that particular problem.

In conducting this examination, I've tried to be objective. It is essential to recognize that the lotteries, in the absence of a destructive scandal, are here to stay. It is just as important to acknowledge that lotteries have had some undeniable, though limited, benefits. Lottery revenues have eased some budget pressures, and to a limited degree, allowed for the real expansion of some worthwhile programs. But these benefits have only been realized at a cost—a cost that is becoming increasingly heavier when measured in terms of existing abuses, potential exploitation that must come with a system driven by the imperative for increased revenue, and the risk of budgetary disorder inherent in the advance appropriation of speculative income.

In return for the rather modest sums received, we have allowed ourselves to become dependent on this extremely regressive form of taxation. The time has arrived to start correcting this addiction to extracting the heaviest burdens from those least able to pay. Left unchecked, our current dependency could easily become an enslavement to flawed and risky public policies.

By way of summary, let's review what a model lottery operation might look like. First, it would look like and act like the game that it is supposed to be, and not like a golden goose being force-fed by the states. This could be brought about by the implementation of the reforms suggested in the final chapters of this work. Those reforms were grouped under subject headings, without sufficient emphasis either on priority or on political feasibility. So in this recapitulation I will try to place them in the order of importance that I believe they warrant, and offer an opinion on how realistic it is to anticipate political acceptance of each respective recommendation.

Priority one. Separate the operational responsibilities and the regulatory functions that are presently merged in all state-run lotteries. Revenue needs permeate, indeed dominate, every decision that is presently made. This situation is not only awkward but creates inherent conflicts of interest and murky ethical judgments. Divorcing the regulatory functions from the day-to-day operations of the games themselves will permit a regulatory perspective that is independent from the purely revenue-raising dynamic. This proposal should meet with little resistance. Inertia might be its most serious opposition.

Priority two. Change the present budget procedures that anticipate lottery revenues and, thereby, force state officials to adopt marketing tactics that will justify their projections. Prophesies are being fulfilled only at the cost of using very questionable practices. The money lust can be short-circuited by permitting lottery receipts to be spent only after they are collected rather than before they are actually in hand. This change will be extremely difficult to accomplish. There will be trauma in the year the change is made. A reasonable political compromise is to provide that the budget anticipate no increase from the previous year's actual receipts. While change might be predictably difficult, a year or two of a lottery not meeting its projected growth would serve as a powerful catalyst for this reform.

Priority three. Modify the avarice of the states as presently evidenced by the regressivity of the implied tax or take-out rate. This can be accomplished by the following:

A. Raise the payouts, providing for more winners in each and every game. The maximum that the states should excise from the gross sales should be set at 32 percent, the highest rate presently in effect for the federal income tax.

B. Intensify marketing to an upper-scale income segment, and eschew present policies which undeniably concentrate only on the lower end of the economic ladder.

C. Provide for the distribution of a percentage of the net proceeds of the game back to the locale wherein the sales originated. At least 25 percent of the states' take-out should go back to the towns in direct ratio to the level of participation taking place in those towns.

Candidly, these reforms are the most difficult to accomplish from a political perspective.

Priority four. The independent regulatory agencies should proscribe abusive marketing techniques that create and compound the highly regressive nature of the present operations. Among the marketing and promotional guidelines that such agencies should adopt are the following:

A. Ban all efforts to encourage antisocial, impulse-oriented, abuse-vulnerable marketing devices, particularly betting by phone.

B. Ban the use of sophisticated or exotic betting by use of videos, automated machines, and so forth. These machines are only ways of cutting overhead by cutting employment.

C. Use the bargaining power of the states to make the lottery operations more, rather than less, labor-intensive. Award lucrative franchises to those who agree to hire the handicapped and disadvantaged rather than those who will cut their commissions.

D. Recognize that oversaturation is both counterproductive and exploitative. Limit the number of terminals, not by use of statewide ratios (which are grossly misleading), but by ratios based on data contained in the federal census tracts, which more accurately reflect how and where lotteries are being marketed in an overly aggressive manner.

E. Forbid the use of betting on the lottery by use of credit cards, and interdict the potential of the state extending credit, or opening gambling bank accounts for the players.

These reforms will be criticized on the grounds that the states should allow the marketplace to operate freely, and that such restrictions will stifle growth. I would expect heated and protracted political debate, followed by eventual adoption of the majority of these regulations.

Priority five. This same independent regulatory agency should also monitor and regulate all advertising policies. The guidelines suggested here are relatively simple and straightforward. The reason they aren't presently honored is because the lotteries are revenue-driven without any consideration of the potential consequences. The guidelines recommended are:

A. No bashing of the work ethic in ads paid for by the state.

B. No intensification of advertising timed to coincide with the mailing of Social Security checks and other entitlement payments.

C. No fantasy nonsense. If the game is just fun and fair, then that is really enough. The state doesn't have to seduce people into a dream world.

D. No tearjerkers, designed to make people think that if they don't play, some needful group will have their needs left unattended.

E. Spread the budget to ensure that all markets are targeted equally, as opposed to the present concentration on the bottom of the income scale.

F. No use of visuals that exploit the elderly, the handicapped, or the young.

In the autumn of 1988, the New Jersey Senate passed, on a narrow vote, legislation banning all advertising by the state's lottery. While unlikely to win similar approval by the Assembly or endorsement by the governor, the senate's action reflects mounting political pressure for reform in the area of advertising. The battle is just starting, and unless some self-restraint is evidenced very quickly, there will be increased pressure on legislatures throughout the country to do something. As stated earlier, I feel that the outright ban on lottery advertising is too severe, and, therefore, unrealistic. The reforms I advocate represent a plausible solution, and I think it is safe to say we will see the reigning-in of lottery advertising along these lines, or similar lines, in the near future.

A cardinal rule in politics is "if it ain't broke, don't fix it." The lotteries are like a sports car designed to carry a minimum load. That sports car isn't exactly broke yet; in fact, we're getting some decent miles out of it. But, when you look a little closer you notice that the brake linings are severely worn, the tires don't have as much tread as they should, and, worst of all, the shocks and springs are so shot that the axles are starting to bend as a result of continual overloading. It may not be broke, but it certainly needs less abuse, and major overhaul.

In politics, the normal catalysts for change are exposed corruption or fiscal crisis. I hope that with the lotteries good judgment and common sense will be enough. Surely, they are all it should take to recognize that you can't use a sports car as a garbage truck, and not expect that someday it would break.

INDEX

Advertising, 72–74, 87-88; budgets for, 75–76; Code of Ethics, 81–82; and First Amendment, 85–86; public service ads, 83–84; reform of, 108–112; and work ethic, 77–79. *See also* Marketing

Advertising Code of Ethics, 81–82

Aggregate tax, 43

Alaska, 19, 20, 38

Allison Jackson Associates, 39

American Newspaper Publishers Association, 85

"An Economic Appraisal of State Lotteries" (Brinner & Clotfelder), 45

Annual installments, 44

Annuity payments, 44

Asimov, Isaac, 101

Athens (Periclean), 12–13

Balanced budgets, 28

Baltimore, Md., 58

Baltimore City, Md., 39

Barrett, David, 39

Belletire, Michael, 96

Bible, 14–15

Blanchard, James, 99

Book of the Abacus (Fibonacci), 101

Borges, George Luis, 12

Brinner, Roger E., 45

Budget process reform, 98–100

California, 22, 33, 48, 57; education budget cuts, 95–96; lottery advertising, 72–73, 76

Canada, 39, 75–76

Caputo, Steven, 51

Casino Act (N.J.), 49

Casino industry, 30, 49

Catchment area, 55

Censorship, definition of, 109

Chain operations, 61–62

Circuit breaking, 93

Clark, David, 103

Clotfelder, Charles T., 42, 45

Code numbers, 68

Colorado, 24, 61–62

Commissions, 61–62, 65–67

Compulsive gambler, 104

Connecticut, 21, 43

Cook, Philip J., 42

Credit cards, 68

Credits, 93

Daily numbers games, 59

Delaware, 33, 57–58, 79

Delaware Council on Gambling Problems, 57–58

Deukmejian, George, 72–73

Direct marketing, 103

District of Columbia, 24, 59, 76

Division of Gaming Enforcement, 49, 50

Dworin, Paul, 100

Eagleton Institute of Politics, 40

Electronic marketing, 104

Enforcement, 49–53, 105–106

Excise rates, 45

Exxon, 29

Federal aid, 20–21

Federal Trade Commission (FTC), 85

Fibonacci, Leonardo, 101–102

Fibonacci Quarterly, 101

First Amendment, 85, 109

Float, 68

Florida, 22, 33

Forbes 500, 29

France, 92

Gaming and Wagering Business, 52, 57, 58, 75, 76, 100, 102

Governing, 32, 41, 51, 52, 59

Grass-roots support, 65

Harwood, Richard, 86

Heisenberg, Werner, 84

Hispanics, 80

Honig, Bill, 95–96

Hosker, Jim, 102

IBM, 29

Illinois, 21, 25, 33, 76, 96

Iowa, 59

Jefferson, Thomas, 11

Jingles, 77

Journal of the Institute for Socioeconomic Studies, 78

Kaplan, H. Roy, 78

Knapp, Elaine S., 52

Koza, John R., 41

LaFluer, Terri, 52

Landers, Ann, 74

Leonardo of Pisa. *See* Fibonacci, Leonardo

Los Angeles *Times,* 42, 82

"Lottery in Babylon, The" (Borges), 12

"Lottery Winners and Work Committment: A Behavioral Test of the American Work Ethic" (Kaplan), 78

Lotto, 25, 27

Louisiana, 19, 20, 22
Lump-sum payments, 44

Marketing: direct, 103; electronic, 104; outlet distribution practices, 54–63; reform of, 101–107; and technology, 64–71. *See also* Advertising
Marrow, Barbara, 51, 76
Maryland, 33, 57, 95; advertising budget, 76; marketing study, 39–43; outlet distribution, 58
Massachusetts, 20, 21, 25, 33, 57, 97
Mexico, 92
Miami *Herald,* 95–96
Michigan, 33, 99–100
Mikesell, John L., 31, 32, 42
Montana, 19
Montgomery County, Md., 39
Mote, Robert L., 23–24

National Association of State Lotteries, 81
National Conference of State Legislatures, 38
National Tax Journal, 45
Nevada, 49
Newark *Star-Ledger,* 40, 51, 76
New Castle County, Delaware, 79
New Hampshire, 21, 27, 38, 60, 92, 102; out-of-state subscriptions, 103
New Jersey, 21, 25, 27, 31–33, 49; lottery advertising, 95; lottery market studies, 39–42; lottery outlet distribution, 59
New Jersey Casino Control Commission, 49–50
New Jersey Lottery Commission, 40, 50, 59
New Jersey Public Broadcasting, 86
New Jersey State Lottery Planning Commission, 11
New York, 20, 21, 25, 27, 33, 43, 57; lottery advertising, 76; odds of winning, 92; Off Track Betting, 67–68
North Dakota, 19

Odds of winning, 92–93
Off Track Betting (OTB), 67–68
Ohio, 21, 25, 33
Oklahoma, 19
On-line terminals, 25–26
Oregon, 51
Outlet distribution, 58–62, 106
Out-of-state subscriptions, 103

Pay-outs, 92–93
Pennsylvania, 11, 25, 33
People's Republic of China, 17
Player-activated terminal, 62
Players, profile of, 38–39
Poincaré, Jules Henri, 12
Professional gamblers, 93–94
Public Administration Review, 31
Public convenience, concept of, 55
Public Gaming, 24, 41
Public service ads, 83–84

Puerto Rico, 92
Puncke, Martin M., 45

Ratekin, Jack, 51
Reagan, Ronald, 20–26
Reaganomics, 20–26
Rebates, 93
Regressive taxes, 30, 37–46
Regulation, 49–53, 105
Response Analysis Corporation, 39
Retailers, 65–66
Retail outlets: distribution of, 58–62, 65
Revenues, 28–29
Rooney, Andy, 77–78
Royal Hong Kong Jockey Club, 64
Russo, Sen. John, 33

Sales taxes, 43
Scientific Games, Inc., 23, 41, 56, 57
Shortfalls, 99
Simonis, Guy, 102
Smith, Adam, 72
Smith, Robert, 51
Solon, 13
Stanek, Edward, 59
State Government News, 51, 52
State income tax, 21–22
"State Lotteries as Fiscal Savior of Fiscal Fraud: A Look at the Evidence" (Mikesell & Zorn), 31
State-operated lotteries, 47–53
Subscription by mail, 69
Suits, Daniel B., 45
Sweepstakes outlets, 102

Tax Reform Act of 1986, 44
Taxes: aggregate, 43; reform of, 91–97; regressive, 30, 37–44; sales, 43; use, 43; vertical equity, 37–38
Technology, 64–71, 103
Telephone sales, 69
Television, 75
Texas, 19, 20, 22
Time value of money, 68–69
Trahan, Edward, 74–75

Use taxes, 43

Van de Kamp, John, 73
Varner, Howard E., 82
Vending machines, 70
Vertical equity, 37–38
Video lottery, 69–70

Washington, 24, 61
Washington *Post,* 86
W. B. Doner & Co., 82
West Virginia, 19
Witt, Elder, 32, 41–42
Work ethic, 77–79
Wyoming, 19, 38

ZAP ad, 82–83
Zorn, C. Kurt, 31, 42